# THE JOY OF LEX

Anyone who has seen him on Channel Four's *Countdown* or heard him on Radio 4's *Just A Minute*, will know that Gyles Brandreth has a special way with words. He is a former Oxford Scholar, President of the Oxford Union, founder of the National Scrabble Championships, European Monopoly Champion and holder of the world records for the longest after-dinner speech (12½ hours), the longest-held screen kiss (3 minutes 33 seconds), the shortest poem in English literature (three words) and the shortest published novel. A columnist for *Woman* and for the Mail on Sunday's *You* Magazine, a scriptwriter and a prolific author, he has been a regular presenter with TV-am since 1983. He lives in London with his wife, three children, two cats and a room full of dictionaries.

Also by Gyles Brandreth and published
by Futura

THE BOOK OF EXCUSES
THE BOOK OF MISTAIKES

# GYLES BRANDRETH

# *The Joy of LEX*

*An amazing and amusing
Z to A and A to Z of words*

ILLUSTRATED BY GEORGE MORAN

Futura

A Futura Book

First published in Great Britain in 1987 by
Robson Books Ltd, London

This edition published in 1988 by Futura Publications,
a Division of Macdonald & Co (Publishers) Ltd,
London & Sydney

ISBN 0 7088 4058 2

Printed and bound in Great Britain by
Cox & Wyman Ltd, Reading

Futura Publications
A Division of
Macdonald & Co (Publishers) Ltd
Greater London House
Hampstead Road
London NW1 7QX
A member of Maxwell Pergamon Publishing Corporation plc

# Contents

## Acknowledgments

I am greatly indebted to my fellow wordaholics Dave Crossland, Michael Curl, Clive Dickinson, Roger Millington and Peter Newby for their contributions to the book. I would also like to thank Dr Frederick C. Mish, editorial director of G. and C. Merriam Company, publishers of Merriam-Webster Dictionaries, for his help and for that of his colleagues. Above all I must thank my friend Darryl Francis for his multifarious contributions, several of which were based on articles of his which originally appeared in *Word Ways: The Journal of Recreational Linguistics*, published by Ross Eckler, Morristown, New Jersey. This edition of *The Joy of Lex* is based on *More Joy of Lex*, published by William Morrow & Co. in New York in 1982, substantially revised by me in London in 1987.

Grateful acknowledgment is made for permission to use the following: In TERSE VERSE Five pun-poems by Alan F.G. Lewis from *A Pun My Soul*, 1977. © Alan F.G. Lewis. / Two clerihews by E. Clerihew Bentley from *The Complete Clerihews of E. Clerihew Bentley*. Oxford University Press, 1981. © E. Clerihew Bentley. / Three poems by Louis Phillips, 1981. © Louis Phillips. / Poetic printout from *Why didn't I think of that?*

# INTRODUCTION

No matter how eloquently a dog may bark, he cannot tell you that his parents were poor but honest.

—BERTRAND RUSSELL

Words and the way we use them are what make us human animals unique. And words and what we can do with them are what *The Joy of Lex* is all about. It is a light-hearted celebration of our language—in my view the richest, most diverse, most exciting and most *entertaining* language in the world.

I know all about the diversity of our language because I'm a devotee of dictionaries. To find the words to fill the pages that follow I've needed to dip into quite a range of them. For example, I've consulted unabridged dictionaries, such as:

*The Oxford English Dictionary* (1933)

*The Supplement to the Oxford English Dictionary* (1972–86)

*Webster's Third New International Dictionary* (published 1961)

*Webster's New International Dictionary,* second edition (1934)

*Webster's New International Dictionary,* first edition (1909)

*The Random House Dictionary,* unabridged edition (1965)

*The Century Dictionary,* and Supplement (1889)

Other English language dictionaries, such as:

*Webster's Ninth New Collegiate Dictionary* (1983)

*A Dictionary of New English* (by Barnhart, Steinmetz and Barnhart, 1973)

*The Second Barnhart Dictionary of New English* (same authors, 1980)

Specialist dictionaries, such as:

*The English Dialect Dictionary* (by Wright, 1905)

*Dorland's Illustrated Medical Dictionary,* 24th edition (1965)

*The American Thesaurus of Slang* (by Berrey and van den Bark, 1954)

*Abbreviations Dictionary,* international edition (by de Sola, 1969)

*An Archaic Dictionary* (by Cooper, 1876)

Biographical and proper name dictionaries, such as:

*Webster's Biographical Dictionary* (1970)

*A Dictionary of Universal Biography* (by Hyamson, second edition, 1951)

*A Dictionary of British Surnames* (by Reaney, 1958)

Geographical dictionaries and gazetteers, such as:

*The Times Index Gazetteer of the World* (1965)

*Gazetteer of the British Isles* (by Bartholomew, 1966)

*Rand McNally Commercial Atlas and Marketing Guide* (98th edition, 1967)

Though the gamut of my reading has been wide—from *The*

*Handbook of American Indians North of Mexico* (Hodge, 1905 and 1965) to *Finnegans Wake* (Joyce, 1939)—and I have drawn on some indisputably scholarly sources, I still feel a trifle nervous about *The Joy of Lex*. I suppose, like most authors, I'm insecure. I've been feeling particularly tentative since I heard the story of the young writer who wasn't. This over-confident youth plagued a prominent editor with relentless requests to read his latest manuscript. Eventually, and reluctantly, the publisher agreed. Two days later he received a cable from the impatient young writer:

MUST HAVE IMMEDIATE DECISION AS OTHER IRONS IN FIRE.

The publisher wired back:

SUGGEST YOU EXTRACT IRONS AND INSERT MANUSCRIPT.

Whatever I feel about the book as a whole, this one page I'm not worried about because while researching *The Joy of Lex* I learnt that 86 per cent of readers never look at introductions. Naturally I respect minority groups, which is why I'm gratified you're one of the 13 per cent reading this now, but the journey through the amazing highways of our language really starts over the page.

All the other wordaholics and verbivores are there already. Why don't we join them?

# Z

## TO A AND BACK AGAIN

### FROM Z TO A

Welcome to the weird and wonderful world of words, a world that depends for its existence entirely on the letters of the alphabet, each one of which happens to be a word in its own right.

Some letters even have several meanings. Here are just twenty-six of them:

Z A buzzing sound.

Y A principal railway track and two diverging branches arranged like the letter Y.

X A mistake or error.

W A printer's type for reproducing the letter W.

V A V-shaped neck of a dress, sweater or blouse.

U Characteristic of the upper classes.

| | |
|---|---|
| *T* | An offensive soccer formation. |
| *S* | A grade assigned by a teacher rating a student's work as satisfactory. |
| *R* | One of the three Rs (writing, reading and arithmetic). |
| *Q* | The ratio of the reactance to the resistance of an oscillatory circuit. |
| *P* | The chemical symbol for phosphorus. |
| *O* | Zero. |
| *N* | An indefinite number. |
| *M* | An antigen of human blood that shares a common genetic locus with the N antigen. |
| *L* | An elevated railroad (US). |
| *K* | In mathematics, a unit vector parallel to the z-axis. |
| *J* | In mathematics, a unit vector parallel to the y-axis. |
| *I* | An excessively egotistic person. |
| *H* | Something having the shape of the letter H. |
| *G* | A sum of 1,000 dollars (US). |
| *F* | A grade assigned by a teacher rating a student's work as so inferior as to be failing. |
| *E* | The second class Lloyd's rating for the quality of a merchant ship. |
| *D* | A semicircle on a pool table that is about twenty-two inches in diameter and is used especially in snooker games. |
| *C* | A sum of 100 dollars (US). |
| *B* | A motion picture produced on a small budget and usually shown as a supplement to the main feature. |
| *A* | A chiefly Scots form of *all*. |

## FROM A TO Z

If you didn't care for those words, try these:

| | |
|---|---|
| *A* | A major blood group. |
| *B* | In men's pyjama sizes, medium. |

| | |
|---|---|
| C | The cardinal number of the set of all real numbers. |
| D | A proportional brassiere cup size, smaller than DD and larger than C. |
| E | A flag bearing the letter E, for "efficiency", presented during World War II as an award by the army or navy to factories meeting or passing their production schedules of war materials. |
| F | The medieval Roman numeral for 40. |
| G | The fifth tone in the scale of C major, or the seventh tone in the relative minor scale, A minor. |
| H | The horizontal component of the Earth's magnetic field. |
| I | The imaginary number that is the square root of minus 1. |
| J | The medieval Roman numeral for 1. |
| K | In computer technology, the number 1000 or 1024. |
| L | An extension at right angles to one end of a building. |
| M | A printing unit. |
| N | In optics, the index of refraction. |
| O | The exclamation oh. |
| P | In music, softly. |
| Q | In Biblical criticism, the symbol for material common to the gospels of Matthew and Luke that was not derived from the gospel of Mark. |
| R | Are (as in "oysters R in season"). |
| S | The energy state of an electron in an atom having an orbital angular momentum of zero. |
| T | The relation between points and closed sets in topological space. |
| U | A Burmese title of respect applied to a man. |
| V | The symbol of allied victory in World War II. |
| W | The twenty-third in order. |
| X | A film recommended for adults only. |
| Y | In mathematics, the y-axis. |
| Z | The medieval Roman numeral for 2000. |

## TWO'S COMPANY

And if single-letter words leave you cold, don't worry. Most of
the words in the book are a little longer – like these:

| | |
|---|---|
| *aa* | A type of volcanic lava. |
| *ag* | Relating to agriculture. |
| *ai* | A South American sloth. |
| *bu* | A Japanese coin. |
| *da* | A heavy Burmese knife. |
| *dy* | A type of sediment deposited in some lakes. |
| *ea* | A stream. |
| *fu* | An administrative division of China and Japan. |
| *fy* | An interjection. |
| *gi* | A costume worn for judo or karate. |
| *gu* | A kind of violin used in the Shetland Islands. |
| *ie* | A mat or basket made from a certain type of fibre. |
| *io* | A large hawk from Hawaii. |
| *ix* | The axle of a cart or wagon. |
| *jo* | A sweetheart. |
| *ka* | A personality double. |
| *ki* | Any of several Asian and Pacific trees. |
| *li* | A Chinese unit of measure. |
| *ob* | An objection. |
| *od* | A force. |
| *oe* | A whirlwind. |
| *om* | A mantra. |
| *oo* | An extinct Hawaiian bird. |
| *ri* | A Japanese unit of measure. |
| *sy* | A chiefly dialectal spelling of *scythe*. |
| *ug* | A feeling of disgust. |
| *vi* | A Polynesian tree. |
| *yi* | In Chinese philosophy, the faithful performance of one's specified duties to society. |

*yu*   Jade.

*zo*   A type of Asian cattle.

## FROM ALOHA TO ZIZZ

These twenty-six words are longer still, and what's interesting about them is that each one begins and ends with the same letter.

| | | |
|---|---|---|
| aloha | *Jernej* | *syllables* |
| blob | *kick* | *tot* |
| cynic | *lull* | *unau* |
| dad | *mum* | *valv* |
| ewe | *neon* | *wow* |
| fluff | *octavo* | *Xerox* |
| grinning | ,*pop* | *yolky* |
| health | *Qaraqalpaq* | *zizz* |
| iambi | *razor* | |

*Iambi* is the plural of *iambus*, part of a line of poetry having two syllables; *Jernej* is a Yugoslavian forename; *Qaraqalpaq* is a Turkic people of Central Asia; *unau* is an animal, a type of sloth; *valv* is a reformed spelling of *valve*.

## WORD CHAIN CHALLENGE

Think of a word beginning with A and ending with B. Think of a word beginning with B and ending with C. Think of a word beginning with C and ending with D. And go on right through the alphabet. Any word will do to fill each gap. How far can you get before you run into trouble? As far as I – J in my case. Look:

| | | | | |
|---|---|---|---|---|
| a__b | *adverb* | c__d | *cold* |
| b__c | *basic* | d__e | *dove* |

| | | | | |
|---|---|---|---|---|
| e—f | elf | | p—q | ??? |
| f—g | flag | | q—r | queer |
| g—h | girth | | r—s | rats |
| h—i | Hindi | | s—t | sit |
| i—j | ??? | | t—u | tableau |
| j—k | junk | | u—v | ??? |
| k—l | kill | | v—w | vow |
| l—m | loom | | w—x | wax |
| m—n | moon | | x—y | xerography |
| n—o | nuncio | | y—z | yez |
| o—p | overlap | | z—a | zebra |

There are three gaps (i—j, p—q, and u—v). These can all be filled by choosing uncommon proper names. For example, *Igej* is a town in Hungary; and *Inathganj* is a place in Pakistan; *Pontacq* is a wine from the south of France; and *Ulanov* and *Ushpitov* are towns in the USSR. *Yez*, by the way, is an Anglo-Irish pronoun meaning "you" in the plural.

## A TO Z IN THE MIDDLE

Here are three lists of words. In each list, the middle letters of the words run from A to Z. In the case of the seven-letter words, the first three letters and the last three letters also form words; in the case of the nine-letter words, the first four letters and the last four letters also form words; and in the case of the eleven-letter words, the first five letters and the last five letters form words. Unfortunately examples of nine and eleven-letter words with a Q in the middle are missing. Yes, even in *The Joy of Lex* there are going to be occasional disappointments.

| 7 LETTERS | 9 LETTERS | 11 LETTERS |
|---|---|---|
| carAvan | bungAlows | blockAdings |
| jawBone | rainBowed | underBought |
| teaCher | blueCoats | extraCtable |
| banDits | snowDrift | screwDriver |

| 7 LETTERS | 9 LETTERS | 11 LETTERS |
|-----------|-----------|------------|
| vetEran | bothEring | adultErated |
| warFare | goldFinch | satinFlower |
| bagGage | kiloGrams | underGround |
| witHout | brigHtens | unrigHtable |
| manIkin | handIwork | deterIorate |
| conJure | flapJacks | interJangle |
| weeKend | sparKling | underKeeled |
| lowLand | paneLwork | oversLoping |
| barMaid | clayMores | blackMailed |
| furNace | lameNtory | heaveNwards |
| bayOnet | bestOwing | trampOlines |
| ramPart | tramPling | enterPrises |
| ubiQuit | ??? | ??? |
| curRant | mayoRship | butteRflies |
| penSion | brimStone | sweepStakes |
| vanTage | sideTrack | forgeTtable |
| bitUmen | consUlate | prestUdying |
| canVass | disaVowed | extraVagate |
| hogWash | bushWomen | lightWeight |
| manXman | trioXides | overeXpress |
| copYcat | pansYlike | staphYlions |
| manZana | waltZlike | hydraZonium |

# Y OUR VERY GOOD HEALTH

If you need an excuse for a drink, you are going to like this chapter. It's the only one in the book I won't allow you to read until you have a drink in your hand – albeit an innocent glass of orange juice. Not only do I want you to enjoy yourself with some liquid refreshment before reading any further, I also want you to read the chapter standing up. Why? Because, ladies and gentlemen, I am about to propose a toast – or to be more accurate I'm about to propose fifteen – so I hope you've got strong legs and you're feeling thirsty.

Once upon a time, when a toast was proposed it was done with wit and charm and style. That isn't true anymore and it's because I want to revive the best of the good old days that I'd like to introduce you to my all-time favourite toasts. Whatever the occasion – a banquet at the Mansion House, a wedding anniversary, a modest meal with two or three friends – you should be able to find something here to fit the bill. So, without more ado, would you kindly raise your glasses and be upstanding, for the Toasts:

1  To your good health, old friend,
   may you live for a thousand years,
   and I be there to count them.

2  May your joys be as deep as the ocean
   and your sorrows as light as its foam.

3  Drink not to my past, which is
            weak and indefensible,
   Nor to my present, which is not
            above reproach,
   But let us drink to our futures, which,
            thank God, are immaculate.

4  Here's wishing you the kind of troubles
   that will last as long as your New Year's resolutions!

5  Here's to the lasses we've loved, my lad,
   Here's to the lips we've pressed;
   For of kisses and lasses
   Like liquor in glasses,
   The last is always the best.

6  Here's to the bride that is to be,
   Happy and smiling and fair,
   Here's to those who would like to be
   And wondering when and where.

7  May I present you to a person who knows
   all there is to know about banks except breaking
   and entering.

8  Here's champagne to our real friends,
   and real pain to our sham friends.

9  Drink! for you know not whence you come, nor why:
   Drink! for you know not why you go, nor where.

10 Drink to me only with thine eyes,
            And I will pledge with mine;
   Or leave a kiss but in the cup
            And I'll not look for wine.

11 Here's to matrimony, the high sea for which
   no compass has yet been invented.

12  Here's to the red of the holly berry,
And to its leaf so green;
And here's to the lips that are just as red,
And the fellow who's not so green.

13  The Ladies – We admire them for their beauty,
respect them for their intelligence, adore them
for their virtue, and love them because we
can't help it.

14  May friendship, like wine, improve as
time advances, and may we always have old wine,
old friends, and young cares.

I've left my favourite toast till last. It was first proposed by Mark Twain.

15  Let us toast the fools; but for them
the rest of us could not succeed.

# X MARKS THE SPOT

### THE JOY OF X

I like some letters of the alphabet much more than others. An analyst – if I had one – could probably tell me why, but I can't. All I know is that I don't care much for J and R, but X I just adore!

Xan is my son's second name and X is the first letter I turn to when I open a new dictionary. Everyone is familiar with xylophone and X-ray and xenophobia, but there are many more intriguing words that begin with X. Here are thirty of the more unusual:

| | |
|---|---|
| *xanorphica* | A stringed musical instrument. |
| *Xanthippe* | An ill-tempered woman. |
| *xanthocyanopsy* | Colour-blindness in which the ability to distinguish only yellow and blue is present, vision for red being wanting. |

| | |
|---|---|
| *xanthoderm* | A person with yellow skin. |
| *xarque* | Dried meat. |
| *xat* | A carved pole erected as a memorial to the dead by some Indians of western North America. |
| *xebec* | A Mediterranean sailing ship. |
| *xenagogue* | A guide. |
| *xenalasy* | The banishment of aliens from ancient Sparta by official action. |
| *xenia* | Gifts sometimes given compulsorily to medieval rulers and churches. |
| *xenodocheionology* | The lore of hotels and inns. |
| *xeriff* | A gold coin, at one time current in Turkey and Egypt. |
| *xerophagy* | The eating of dry food. |
| *xerosis* | Abnormal dryness of a body. |
| *xibalba* | In Maya religion, the abode of the dead. |
| *xicaque* | An Indian people of northern Honduras. |
| *xilinous* | Of cotton. |
| *xiphoid* | Sword-shaped. |
| *xoanon* | A primitive image carved in wood. |
| *xu* | A monetary unit of North Vietnam. |
| *xurel* | A fish |
| *xya* | A genus of mole-crickets, mainly tropical. |
| *xylanthrax* | Charcoal. |
| *xyloglyphy* | Artistic wood carving. |
| *xylomancy* | Divination by means of pieces of wood. |
| *xylopolist* | A timber merchant. |
| *xylosistron* | A musical instrument. |
| *xysma* | Membranous shreds in the stools of patients with diarrhoea or dysentery. |
| *xyster* | An instrument for scraping bones. |
| *xystus* | A walk lined with trees. |

## THE CRUX OF THE MATTER

There are many more words that end with X than start with it. I have scoured the dictionaries to come up with twenty-six of the longest, each beginning with a different letter of the alphabet. Some of the definitions are obvious, but several are quite as obscure as the words themselves. So if you want them I'll leave you to leaf through the pages of the *Oxford English Dictionary*, *Webster's* and whatever else you wish to try.

archcystosyrinx

blennothorax

coadministratix

dispensatrix

erysipalothrix

fornicatrix

glossenthrax

hydropneumothorax

impersonatrix

janitrix

knisteneaux

lithanthrax

metrosalpinx

negotiatrix

odontopteryx

pneumohydrothorax

quadruplex

rickettsialpox

seropneumothorax

trophothylax

ultraorthodox

versificatrix

wheelbox

xylanthrex

yunx

zelatrix

## The joy of lex

If X is my favourite letter, *lex* is almost my favourite three-letter word. I reckon there are about fifty words in the English language that begin with the letters L, E, X. Here are thirty of them:

| | |
|---|---|
| *Lexa* | A town in Arkansas, USA. |
| *Lexden* | A town in Essex. |
| *lexeme* | A meaningful speech form that is an item of the vocabulary of a language. |
| *lexemic* | Relating to a lexeme. |
| *lexer* | A student of law. |
| *lexia* | A soft raisin produced chiefly in Spain and Australia. |
| *lexica* | A plural of *lexicon*. |
| *lexical* | Relating to words or the vocabulary of a language. |
| *lexicalize* | To accept into the vocabulary of a language. |
| *lexicographer* | A dictionary compiler. |
| *lexicographian* | Relating to lexicography. |
| *lexicographical* | Relating to lexicography. |
| *lexicography* | The principles and practices of dictionary making. |
| *lexicological* | Relating to lexicology. |
| *lexicologist* | One versed in lexicology. |
| *lexicology* | The science of the derivation and significance of words. |
| *lexicon* | A dictionary or word-stock. |
| *lexiconist* | A compiler of a lexicon. |
| *lexiconize* | To make a lexicon. |
| *lexicostatistic* | Pertaining to the statistics of vocabulary. |
| *lexigram* | Any figure or symbol used to represent a word. |
| *lexigraphic* | Pertaining to lexigraphy. |
| *lexigraphy* | The art or practice of defining words. |

| | |
|---|---|
| *Lexington* | A town in Massachusetts, the site of the first engagement of the American Revolution. |
| *lexiphanes* | A phrase monger. |
| *lexiphanic* | Pretentious. |
| *lexiphanicism* | Pretentious phraseology. |
| *lexipharmic* | An antidote. |
| *lexis* | The wording of a piece of writing. |

And here are the last three letters of thirty words that end with L, E, X. Can you work out how the words should begin? (See Answers on page 258.)

| | |
|---|---|
| — — — — lex | To strike with a sudden loss of consciousness. |
| — — — — — — — lex | An accent mark. |
| — — — — lex | Complicated. |
| — — lex | A genus of mosquitoes. |
| — — — — — — lex | Having ten parts. |
| — — — lex | Twofold. |
| — — — lex | Without legal authority. |
| — lex | To bend. |
| — — — — — — — lex | 10 raised to the power of a googol. |
| — — — lex | Man's great toe. |
| — lex | An evergreen oak of southern Europe. |
| — — — lcx | Intricate. |
| — — — — — — lex | Having numerous parts. |
| — — — — — lex | Relating to a system of telegraphy in which eight messages can be sent simultaneously. |
| — — — — lex | To bewilder. |
| — lex | To make like a network. |
| — — — lex | Thumb. |
| — — — — lex | A complicated network of nerves. |

| | | |
|---|---|---|
| — — lex | | A genus of fleas. |
| — — — — — — lex | | Relating to a specific system of telegraphy. |
| — — — lex | | An act performed automatically. |
| — — — — — lex | | Bend abruptly backward. |
| — — — lex | | The head of a tapeworm. |
| — — lex | | A pure form of silica. |
| — — — — lex | | Single. |
| — — — — — lex | | Furniture. |
| — — lex | | A communication service. |
| — — — — lex | | Threefold. |
| — lex | | A genus of spiny shrubs. |
| — — — — — — lex | | Simple. |

## COMPLEX ARRANGEMENTS

Here are thirty more words that don't seem to have anything to do with Lex – yet. This is where you come in. Take each word in turn, add the letters *L, E* and *X*, and rearrange all the letters to make a new word. For example, if *TO* was in the list, add the letters *LEX*, rearrange all five, and make the new word EXTOL. Simple, isn't it?

| | | |
|---|---|---|
| at | flyer | ropiest |
| coin | goosy | seat |
| cosier | hi | shop |
| cued | hoof | sienna |
| dart | linky | snary |
| date | lot | sup |
| dope | mawl | taut |
| due | pain | ties |
| eater | pore | upset |
| fan | read | us |

(See Answers on page 258.)

## TWO OUT OF THREE

You can change the vowel in the middle of *lex* and come up with four other useful words:

| | |
|---|---|
| *lax* | Not strict. |
| *lix* | A Roman camp follower. |
| *lox* | Liquid oxygen. |
| *lux* | In physics, a unit of illumination. |

(Not to mention *lyx*, which is a combining form, related to the chemical lyxose.)

If you want to change the last letter of lex and come up with a series of alternative three-letter words, each beginning with a different letter of the alphabet, you can – if you don't mind ignoring Q and including slang, abbreviations, dialect, proper names and obsolete words galore.

| | |
|---|---|
| *lea* | Pasture. |
| *leb* | As much liquid or food as can be taken into the mouth or thrown by the hand at one time. |
| *lec* | An obsolete spelling of *leek*. |
| *led* | The past tense of *lead*. |
| *lee* | The side sheltered from the wind. |
| *lef* | An obsolete spelling of *leaf, leave, lief*, and *live*. |
| *leg* | A limb. |
| *Leh* | A commercial town in Ladakh province, Kashmir. |
| *lei* | A Polynesian garland of flowers. |
| *lej* | An abbreviation for *longitudinal expansion joint*. |
| *lek* | A site to which birds regularly resort for the purposes of sexual display and courtship. |
| *lel* | An obsolete spelling of *leal*, "loyal". |
| *LEM* | Lunar excursion module. |
| *Len* | Short for *Leonard*. |
| *Leo* | The fifth sign of the zodiac. |
| *lep* | A dialectal spelling of *lap* and *leap*. |
| *leq* | ??? |

| *Ler* | The Irish god of the sea, the original of King Lear. |
| *les* | An obsolete spelling of *lace, lease, leash*, and *less*. |
| *let* | Allow. |
| *leu* | The basic monetary unit of Romania. |
| *lev* | The basic monetary unit of Bulgaria. |
| *lew* | A place of shelter. |
| *lex* | Law. |
| *ley* | Pasture. |
| *lez* | Slang abbreviation for lesbian. |

Running through the alphabet looking for three-letter words ending in *ex* isn't so easy.

| *Aex* | A genus of short-legged perching duck. |
| *bex* | An obsolete plural of *beak*. |
| *cex* | An obsolete spelling of *six*. |
| *Dex* | A diminutive form of the masculine forename Dexter. |
| *eex* | ??? |
| *fex* | A variant spelling of *fax*, the hair on the head. |
| *gex* | An English dialect word meaning "to guess". |
| *hex* | A spell or jinx. |
| *iex* | ??? |
| *Jex* | A surname, related to Geake and Jacks. |
| *kex* | The dry stalk of various plants. |
| *lex* | Law. |
| *Mex* | A Mexican. |
| *nex* | An obsolete spelling of *next*. |
| *OEX* | An abbreviation for the Office of Educational Exchange. |
| *pex* | An obsolete spelling of *pax*, peace. |
| *qex* | ??? |
| *rex* | King. |
| *sex* | Gender. |
| *Tex* | A nickname for Texas or someone from Texas. |
| *uex* | An obsolete spelling of *vex*. |
| *vex* | To worry. |

| | |
|---|---|
| *wex* | A dialectal spelling of wax. |
| *xex* | ??? |
| *yex* | To hiccup. |
| *zex* | A variant spelling of *sax*, a chopping tool for trimming slates. |

It seems we don't yet have meanings for *eex, iex qex* and *xex*. I believe we ought to have. Perhaps *eex* should be the first spouse of a twice-divorced person, *iex* an English form of "Eureka!", *qex* someone who gets kicks out of spelling badly and *xex* be a point on the map . . . as in "xex marks the spot". If you have any deft definitions of your own, tell your friends. I think we should all do what we can here to spread the words.

# W HAT'S IN A NAME?

## WHAT AM I?

If you don't know who you are, I can't help you. But if you don't know *what* you are, perhaps I can. I know what I am.

Gyles is quite simply the plural form of gyle, and depending on the dictionary you care to consult, gyle is defined as:

—wort in the process of fermentation added to a stout or ale.
—the beer produced at one brewing.
—a quantity of beer brewed at one time.
—a brewing.
—the vat in which the wort is left to ferment.
—an obsolete spelling of *guile*.

—a channel on a beach that the high tide fills, leaving a small island within.
—an island of sand.
—quicksand.
—a ravine, a narrow valley or glen, with precipitous or rocky banks, generally wooded and with a stream running at the bottom.
—a dingle.
—a rivulet or mountain stream.
—the bed of a stream.
—a waterfall.
—a ditch.

And brandreth is variously defined as:

—a gridiron.
—a tripod or trivet of iron.
—a wooden framework for support, as a stand for a small haystack.
—a framework of wood for various purposes, as a stand for a cask.
—a substructure of piles to support a house.
—a fence or rail around the opening of a well.
—an iron framework placed over or before a fire, on which to rest utensils in cooking.
—an iron grating or brazier in which fire is kindled in the open air.
—a wooden or iron arm fixed into the throat of a spindle in a flour mill.
—one of the cross-timbers in a pit, to which slides are bolted.
—a grating placed over the entrance of a drain or sewer.
—the name of a mountain in Cumbria which is 2,344 feet high.
—the name of a community in Herkimer County, New York, named, I believe, after my great-great-grandfather, who marketed Brandreth's Pills, a medicine that could cure almost anything – from headache to heart disease – and made him a fortune. (All since gone, I'm sorry to say.)

Of course, I'm not alone. Numerous surnames have meanings as ordinary words – I know a Butcher and a Baker and I believe there's a man in Florida called Hans Candlestickmaker – and there are plenty of forenames that are also words in their own right. For example, Jenny is a female bird or animal, especially a female donkey; Jemima is an elastic-sided boot; Mike is short for *microphone*; and Will is a document bequeathing one's possessions at death.

Here, with definitions, are more than a hundred of them. I hope you find your name in the list.

| | |
|---|---|
| *Abigail* | A lady's maid. |
| *Albert* | A short kind of watch chain. |
| *Alma* | An Egyptian dancing girl. |
| *Ann* | From 1672 to 1925, a half-year's stipend payable to the wife of a parish minister after his death. |
| *Anna* | An obsolescent coin of India and Pakistan. |
| *Basil* | An aromatic plant. |
| *Ben* | A mountain peak. |
| *Beryl* | A precious stone. |
| *Bertha* | A woman's falling collar. |
| *Beth* | The second letter of the Hebrew alphabet. |
| *Betty* | A burglar's jemmy. |
| *Bill* | A bird's beak. |
| *Billy* | An Australian teapot. |
| *Bob* | To move up and down. |
| *Bobby* | A policeman. |
| *Carol* | A Christmas song. |
| *Cicely* | The name of several plants. |
| *Clement* | Mild. |
| *Clementine* | A type of orange. |
| *Colin* | The Virginian quail. |
| *Craig* | A crag, a rough steep rock or point. |
| *Dan* | A box for carrying coal. |
| *Dick* | A detective. |
| *Dickens* | The devil. |
| *Dicky* | A false shirtfront. |
| *Dolly* | A trolley. |

| | |
|---|---|
| *Don* | To put on. |
| *Emma* | A signaller's name for the letter M. |
| *Eric* | A murderer's fine in old Irish law. |
| *Faith* | Confidence. |
| *Fay* | A fairy. |
| *Flora* | The vegetation of a region. |
| *Frank* | Open. |
| *Grace* | A virtue. |
| *Guy* | An odd figure or fellow. |
| *Hank* | A loop. |
| *Harry* | To harass. |
| *Hazel* | Light brown. |
| *Heather* | A common shrub. |
| *Henry* | In physics, the unit of inductance. |
| *Iris* | Part of the eye. |
| *Ivy* | An evergreen climbing plant. |
| *Jack* | A device for raising heavy weights. |
| *Jake* | A country lout. |
| *James* | A burglar's jemmy. |
| *Jane* | A woman. |
| *Jean* | A twilled cotton cloth. |
| *Jeff* | In circus slang, a rope. |
| *Jerry* | A chamber pot. |
| *Jess* | A short strap around the legs of a hawk. |
| *Jill* | A female ferret. |
| *Jo* | A beloved one. |
| *Joey* | A young kangaroo. |
| *Josh* | To ridicule. |
| *Ken* | To know. |
| *Kirk* | A church. |
| *Laura* | A group of recluses' cells. |
| *Louis* | An old French gold coin. |
| *Luke* | Tepid. |
| *Madge* | A magpie. |

| | |
|---|---|
| *Maria* | Dark areas on the moon and Mars. |
| *Martin* | A bird. |
| *Matt* | Dull. |
| *Molly* | A milksop. |
| *Mona* | A West African monkey. |
| *Mungo* | Waste cloth. |
| *Nelly* | A large petrel, a type of bird. |
| *Nelson* | A wrestling hold. |
| *Nick* | To steal. |
| *Norma* | A rule or standard. |
| *Norman* | A bar inserted in a windlass. |
| *Olive* | A tree with oily fruit. |
| *Oliver* | A forge hammer worked by hand. |
| *Otto* | A fragrant oil. |
| *Pansy* | The name of various plants. |
| *Patrick* | A seventeenth-century Irish halfpenny. |
| *Patty* | A little pie. |
| *Paul* | An obsolete papal silver coin. |
| *Peggy* | A small warbler, a type of bird. |
| *Peter* | To dwindle away. |
| *Polly* | A tube of mineral water. |
| *Rex* | Pranks. |
| *Rob* | To plunder. |
| *Robin* | A bird with a red-orange breast. |
| *Rose* | Got up. |
| *Rosemary* | A small fragrant shrub. |
| *Ruby* | A highly prized stone. |
| *Ruth* | Pity. |
| *Sally* | To rush out suddenly. |
| *Sam* | Together. |
| *Saul* | A Scots form of *soul*. |
| *Sophia* | Divine wisdom. |
| *Taffy* | Flattery. |
| *Ted* | To spread new-mown grass for drying. |

| | |
|---|---|
| *Terry* | A pile fabric. |
| *Timothy* | A grass for feeding cattle. |
| *Toby* | Robbery on the road. |
| *Tommy* | A private in the British army. |
| *Tony* | Fashionable. |
| *Victor* | A winner. |
| *Wally* | Excellent. |
| *Watt* | In physics, a unit of power. |

## AN ORAL DANGER

"An oral danger" is, of course, an anagram of *Ronald Reagan*. Less controversial – and less telling – are these anagrams of my name:

| | |
|---|---|
| Bet her dry slang | Lady G's brethren |
| Beth's grand lyre | Lend gray berths |
| Blyth's gardener | Lengthy red bars |
| Brash, dry, gentle | Set herb grandly |
| Brethren lag Syd | Sh! Tangled berry |
| Dr. Glen's breathy | St. Henry garbled |
| Dry angel berths | Tangle dry herbs |
| Gentry held bars | The berry glands |
| Gentry's halberd | The dry barn legs |
| Grab thy lenders | The Gerry's bland |
| Hags blend Terry | The grand beryls |
| Harry gets blend | Try garbled hens |

Curiously a great number of forenames are anagrams of other forenames. Look at these:

| | |
|---|---|
| Christiaan, Christiana | Ramona, Romana |
| Carla, Clara | Abbe, Babe, Ebba |
| Adina, Aidan, Nadia, Naida | Barend, Braden, Brande, Brenda |
| Adna, Anda, Dana, Nada | Bernard, Brander |
| Alvina, Lavina | Brady, Darby |
| Armina, Marian, Marina | Embla, Mabel, Mable, Melba |
| Anita, Tania | Albert, Bartel, Bartle |

Bat, Tab
Meriadoc, Mordecai
Alice, Celai, Celia
Caroline, Cornelia
Christian, Christina
Carlo, Carol, Coral
Claus, Lucas
Darel-Gene, Geraldene
Darleen, Darlene, Leander,
Leandre, Learned
Dorothea, Theodora
    Leandro, Leonard
Dean, Dena, Edan, Edna
Waldorf, Walford
Lorinda, Rinaldo, Rolinda
Arnoldo, Orlando
Arnold, Landor, Nordal,
    Roland, Roldan, Ronald
Rosamond, Rosmonda
Andy, Dyna
Stanhope, Stephano
Antoine, Antonie
Jane, Jean
Paulet, Petula
Earl, Lear
Amery, Marye
Warner, Warren
Zane, Zena
Etta, Tate
Gary, Gray

Hatty, Hyatt
Oliva, Viola
Marion, Morina
Mario, Moira
Ian, Ina
Nita, Tina
Lawton, Walton
Norma, Ramon, Roman
Amor, Mora, Omar, Roma
Mary, Myra
Mat, Tam
Amy, May
Ann, Nan
Bert, Bret
Cheri, Erich
Colin, Nicol
Dorothee, Theodore
Delores, Delrose
Edsel, Leeds
Fidel, Field
Dolly, Lloyd
Dot, Tod
Esther, Hester
Ernie, Irene, Renie
Elmer, Merle
Simeon, Simone
Len, Nel
Elon, Leon, Noel, Olen

Believe it or not, the list as given here is arranged in a very specific order. It is *not* a random ordering. It is obviously not alphabetically ordered, nor ordered by length. Can you determine the way in which the list of names has been ordered? (See Answers on page 259.)

# VERBIGERATION

Verbigeration is something of which, as a paid-up member of Wordaholics Anonymous, I hope I'm not guilty. Do you know what it means? I do, but only because I looked it up in *Webster's Third New International Dictionary*, where I found fifty different words connected in some way with the study of words and language, writing, and speech.

Here are the fifty words:

| | |
|---|---|
| 1 agnomen | 7 caconym |
| 2 anaphora | 8 caesura |
| 3 antiphrasis | 9 calque |
| 4 asyndeton | 10 carriwitchet |
| 5 billingsgate | 11 cheville |
| 6 boustrophedon | 12 chrestomathy |

13 coprolalia
14 ambolalia
15 enclitic
16 epexegesis
17 epistrophe
18 equivoke
19 etymon
20 cuonym
21 euphuism
22 gradus
23 hapax
24 heteroclitic
25 idioglossia
26 incipit
27 isogloss
28 jussive
29 koine
30 macaronic
31 metonymy

32 neolalia
33 neoterism
34 onomasiology
35 onomasticon
36 onomatomania
37 orismology
38 palilalia
39 paralalia
40 paraphrasia
41 parasynthesis
42 paroemiology
43 paronym
44 paronomasia
45 periphrasis
46 pleonasm
47 schizophasia
48 semanteme
49 tmesis
50 verbigeration

And here are fifty definitions, but the definitions aren't given in the same order as the words. What you've got to do is match the words to the definitions. If you get as many as thirty correctly matched, you're obviously a dedicated verbivore. If you manage forty, you're probably a lexicographer by profession. And if you get all fifty right, you should be writing the book, not me.

A    A collection or listing of proper names of persons or places.
B    A play upon words in which the same word is used in different senses, or words similar in sound are set in opposition so as to give antithetical force.
C    Speech, especially of a psychotic, that includes words that are new and meaningless to the hearer.
D    The study of words and expressions having similar or associated concepts for being grouped.

E    The subject of proverbs.

F    A word formed from a word in another language.

G    Uncontrollable obsession with words or names or their meanings or their sounds.

H    A newly invented word or phrase.

I    A word or a base that expresses a definite image or idea.

J    A speech disorder marked by distortions of sounds or substitutions of letters.

K    A composition characterized by a mixture of vernacular words with Latin words or with non-Latin words having Latin endings.

L    Continual repetition of stereotyped phrases, as in schizophrenia.

M    A speech defect marked by abnormal repetition of syllables, words, or phrases.

N    The disorganized speech characteristic of schizophrenia.

O    The science of defining technical terms.

P    Speech defect characterized by incoherence in arrangement of words.

Q    The use of a longer phrasing in place of a possible shorter and plainer form of expression.

R    Separation of parts of a compound word by the intervention of one or more words.

S    A break in the flow of sound in a line of verse, occasioned usually by a rhetorical pause and occurring usually at about the middle of the verse.

T    A noun irregular in declension.

U    The use of more words than those necessary to denote mere sense.

V    A figure of speech that consists of using the name of one thing for that of something else with which it is associated.

W    The process of word formation by adding a derivative ending and prefixing a particle (as in *denationalize*).

X    A word or form evidenced by a single citation.

Y    The writing of alternate lines in opposite directions, one line from left to right and the next from right to left.

Z     The interpolation of meaningless sounds or words into speech.

AA     Obsessive or uncontrollable use of obscene language.

BB     Repetition of the same word or expression at the end of successive phrases, clauses, or sentences for rhetorical effect.

CC     Repetition of a word or words at the beginning of two or more successive clauses or verses for rhetorical or poetic effect.

DD     An explanation following a word or larger part of a text that limits its application or clarifies its meaning.

EE     A word or particle treated in pronunciation as forming part of the preceding word (as English *thee* in *prithee* and *not* in *cannot*).

FF     A linguistic feature shared by some but not all speakers of a dialect, a language, or a group of related languages.

GG     A linguistic borrowing that consists of the imitation in one language in some part of the peculiar range of meaning of a particular word in another language.

HH     The use of words in senses opposite to the generally accepted meanings or the use of a word in this way usually for humorous or ironical purposes.

II     A condition in which the affected person pronounces his words so badly as to speak a language of his own.

JJ     A taxonymic name that is objectionable for linguistic reasons.

KK     A hoaxing or riddling question.

LL     A selection of passages from various authors compiled as an aid to learning a language.

MM     A redundant word or phrase used to fill out a sentence or verse.

NN     A word, form, case, or mood expression command.

OO     Wordplay.

PP     The introductory words or part of a medieval manuscript or early printed book.

QQ     An affected style of conversation and writing fashionable in the time of Queen Elizabeth I and characterized by antithesis, alliteration, similes, and a pervading striving for elegance.

RR   A dictionary of Greek or Latin prosody and poetical phrases formerly used as an aid in the writing of poetry in Greek or Latin.

SS   A name well suited to the person, place, or thing named.

TT   A dialect or language of a region, country, or people that has become the common or standard language of a larger area and of other peoples.

UU   The original form of a word either in the same language or in an ancestral language.

VV   An additional name or epithet.

WW   Condemnatory language marked by the coarse or offensive and scornfully abusive or contentious.

XX   Omission of the conjunctions that ordinarily join coordinate words or clauses.

(See Answers on page 259.)

# U NCLES AND AUNTS

It is a mistake to try to put on your uncles and aunts when you are already wearing your Oscar Hocks and your bottles of booze. Your storm and strife will think you're elephant trunk again!

And if that didn't make much sense to you, don't worry. It's in Rhyming Slang, a jargon with an exhilarating, if limited, vocabulary that has been used in America, Australia and Britain for over a hundred years. If you feel like adding a little colour to your everyday language, you could try adopting a few of these unusual but useful words and phrase. All are in current use.

| | |
|---|---|
| *apple and banana* | piano |
| *applepies* | eyes |
| *bacon and eggs* | legs |
| *bar of soap* | dope |

| | |
|---|---|
| *ben flake* | steak |
| *big bloke* | coke (short for cocaine) |
| *bonny fair* | hair |
| *bottles of booze* | shoes |
| *bowl of chalk* | talk |
| *brothers and sisters* | whiskers |
| *bull's aunts* | pants |
| *by the peck* | neck |
| *Catherine Hayes* | long days |
| *chair and cross* | horse |
| *Charlie Beck* | check |
| *Charlie Chalk* | talk |
| *Charlie Horner* | corner |
| *Charlie Rocks* | socks |
| *cocked hat* | rat (an informer) |
| *cracks-a-cry* | die |
| *daisy roots* | boots |
| *Dan O'Leary* | weary |
| *dig and dirt* | shirt |
| *dime a pop* | cop |
| *east-and-west* | vest |
| *elephant trunk* | drunk |
| *fiddle and flute* | suit |
| *fifteen and seven* | heaven (enjoyable) |
| *fine and dandy* | brandy |
| *fleas and ants pants* | pants |
| *frog a log* | dog |
| *garlic and glue* | stew |
| *ginger ale* | jail |
| *grocery store* | door |
| *hair and brain* | chain |
| *hairy float* | coat |
| *hammer and tack* | back (of the body) |
| *hard and flat* | hat |

| | |
|---|---|
| *heart and lung* | tongue |
| *heavenly bliss* | kiss |
| *here and there* | chair |
| *hook of mutton* | button |
| *I declare* | chair |
| *in the sleet* | in the street |
| *ivory float* | coat |
| *Jack Scratch* | match |
| *Jerry McGinn* | chin |
| *Jimmy Hope* | soap |
| *Johnnie Rump* | pump |
| *Johnnie O'Brien* | iron |
| *Johnnie Russell* | hustle |
| *Jollopp* | stop |
| *Kelly Ned* | head |
| *Kennedy Rot* | sot |
| *Kentucky horn* | corn |
| *kiss the cross* | the boss |
| *lard and pail* | jail |
| *leg-rope* | hope |
| *made mile* | smile |
| *moan and wail* | Jall |
| *mother and daughter* | water |
| *mumbley pegs* | legs |
| *Nancy prance* | dance |
| *new south* | mouth |
| *Oh heck* | neck |
| *ones and twos* | shoes |
| *Oscar Hocks* | socks |
| *Oscar Joes* | toes |
| *pair of braces* | races |
| *peaches and pears* | stairs |
| *pint pot* | sot |
| *pot of jelly* | belly |

| | |
|---|---|
| *quarter pot* | sot |
| *rattle and jar* | car |
| *raw and ripe* | pipe |
| *red steer* | beer |
| *ride plush* | to hush |
| *rise and shine* | wine |
| *roasty roast* | post (winning) |
| *rocks and boulders* | shoulders |
| *rolley roar* | floor |
| *roots* | boots |
| *roses red* | bed |
| *ruby rose* | nose |
| *rumble and shock* | knock (on the door) |
| *satin and silk* | milk |
| *scarlet pips* | lips |
| *scream and holler* | dollar |
| *see the shine* | give a dime |
| *sheery flips* | lips |
| *sighs and tears* | ears |
| *silk and top* | cop |
| *silk and twine* | wine |
| *slick and sleeth* | teeth |
| *smack in the eye* | pie |
| *smear and smudge* | judge |
| *south of the equator* | elevator |
| *spinning top* | cop |
| *stand an ale* | go bail (for) |
| *storm and strife* | wife |
| *strong and thin* | gin |
| *stump the chalk* | walk |
| *sweet Margaret* | cigarette |
| *switch and bone* | telephone |
| *tar and feather* | weather |
| *tarry rope* | dope |

| | |
|---|---|
| *tea and tattle* | battle |
| *tears and cheers* | ears |
| *thick and dense* | expense |
| *three or four* | door |
| *tick tack* | track |
| *ting-a-ling* | ring |
| *tip and tap* | cap |
| *toad in the hole* | roll of currency notes |
| *Tommy Rocks* | socks |
| *Tommy Toy* | boy |
| *Tom Noddy* | body |
| *train wreck* | neck |
| *uncles and aunts* | pants |
| *unders and beneaths* | teeth |
| *very best* | chest |
| *whale and gale* | jail |
| *wish me luck* | duck (dodge or escape) |
| *you know* | snow (cocaine) |

# TERSE VERSE

If you write a long sentence,
  Then write down
  Short phrases
  Like lists,
  Is
  It
  Poetry?

No, never, you answer firmly. And I used to agree until I came across the telling terse verse of Alan F.G. Lewis, the world's greatest punster. If this isn't poetry (of a sort), what is?

### Valentine Rhyme

My heart and I
Call to you
But you're too deaf
to Eros.

### Please Be Seated

When she said "Howdah do
Take a pew
You look divan"
I thought "This is sit"
But I was throne aside
When she decided to settle
For a pouffe
A sort of plinth charming
Who promised to support her
For the rest of her dais,
Next time I'll be more chairy.

### The Tree of Love

Yew witch Hazel
It's plane
I'm sycamore poplar girls
And aspen alder time
On the beach
And pine to cedar day
When I maple to say
"Hazel lime yours,
Cumquat may."

### A Musical Marriage

She would keep
Harping on about tidiness
Blowing her own trumpet
And drumming it into me
That I mustn't fiddle
With my hair
I think she was instrumental
In our divorce.

### *I Told Her*

I told her no sensibleman
Would take her dancing
In her bikini
So she went
With a little moron.

### *The Poet's Dilemma*

Once upon a time I used
To mispell
To sometimes split infinitives
To get words of out order
To punctuate, – badly
To confused my tenses
To deem old words wondrous fair
to ignore capitals
To employ common or garden clichés
To miss the occasional out
To indulge in tautological repetitive statements
To exaggerate hundreds of times a day
And to repeat puns quite by chants
But worst of all I used
To forget to finish what I

## CHAPS & MAPS

The Art of Biography
Is different from Geography
Geography is about maps,
But biography is about chaps.

And a versified biography is called a Clerihew. Here are a couple by E. Clerihew Bentley (1875–1956), the man who invented this particular form of poetry:

"I quite realized," said Columbus,
"That the earth was not a rhombus,
But I am a little annoyed
To find it an oblate spheroid."

The great Duke of Wellington
Reduced himself to a skellington,
He reached seven stone two,
And then – Waterloo!

Louis Phillips is a modern master of the art of versified biography. Here are three of his gems:

Robert DeNiro
Is a screen hero.
Only a slob
Would call him Bob.

Clara Bow
(You may know)
Made a hit
By emphasizing It.

John D. Rockefeller made a million.
Oh, hell, he made a billion,
When he turned up soil,
*Voila! Oil!*

And for a poem that's a picture as well as a concise biography in verse, I don't think you could do better than this:

He rocked the boat,
Did Ezra Shrank.
These bubbles mark
O
O
O
O
O
Where Ezra sank.

Here's another short poem that does two things at once. It tells a story and it looks good.

> He went out one lovely night
>     To call upon a miss,
> And when he reached her residence
>               this.
>        like
>     stairs
>    up
>   ran
> He
> Her papa met him at the door,
>     He didn't see the miss.
> He'll not go there again though
>    — for
> He
>    went
>      down
>        stairs
>          like
>           this.

## POETIC INJUSTICE

Some of the most memorable short poems are also the most savage. Here are my six favourite ruthless rhymes. The first is by one of the world's great novelists, William Makepeace Thackeray, author of *Vanity Fair*. The rest are the work of that most prolific (and impoverished) of poets, Anon.

> Charlotte, having seen his body,
> Borne before her on a shutter,
> Like a well-conducted person
> Went on cutting bread and butter.

> Last night I slew my wife,
> Stretched her on the parquet flooring;
> I was loth to take her life,
> But I had to stop her snoring.

O'er the rugged mountain's brow
Clara threw the twins she nursed,
And remarked, "I wonder now
Which will reach the bottom first?"

I had written to Aunt Maud,
        Who was on a trip abroad,
When I heard she'd died of cramp
        Just too late to save the stamp.

"There's been an accident!" they said,
"Your husband's cut in half; he's dead!"
"Indeed!" said Mrs Brown. "Well, if you please
Would you send me the half that's got my keys."

Llewelyn Peter James Maguire,
Touched a live electric wire;
Back on his heels it sent him rocking –
His language (like the wire) was shocking.

## POETIC PRINTOUT

The twenty-first century is almost upon us, and helping us
toward it in fine style is the unique Kay Hines, inventor of the
Sonnet Slot Machine, a device designed to satisfy the poet and
the gambler in us all. According to Ms. Hines:

> This slot machine has, instead of the customary three or four
> windows, fourteen rows of five windows each. In each little
> window, instead of the usual images of lemons, bells, cherries, etc.,
> a word or words appear, comprising an iambic foot for the classic
> fourteen-line pentameter sonnet. When a coin is inserted and the
> handle is pulled, all the words whirl around, stopping randomly to
> form one among potentially thousands of sonnets. There are
> possible combinations that yield the Petrarchan sonnet rhyme
> scheme (with variations between Italian and Sicilian sestet) and
> also the Shakespearean sonnet rhyme scheme. Achieving a perfect
> or near-perfect rhyme scheme returns the player either a jackpot or
> free plays. And every player receives a printout of the sonnet he has
> composed.

If you enjoy truly contemporary poetry you might like this. It was
written by a computer.

How can the purple yeti be so red,
Or chestnuts, like a widgeon calmly groan?
No sheep is quite as crooked as a bed,
Though chickens ever try to hide a bone.
I grieve that greasy turnips slowly march:
Indeed, inflated is the icy pig:
For as the alligator strikes the larch,
So sighs the grazing goldfish for a wig.
Oh, has the pilchard argued with a top?
She never that the parsnip is too weird!
I tell thee that the wolf-man will not hop
And no man ever praised the convex beard.
Effulgent is the day when bishops turn:
So let not the doctor wake the urn!

It may read like nonsense (which it is) but the metre and the rhymes are spot on. It was produced by a computer fed with a long list of words, classified by parts of speech and numbers of syllables.

And if you don't like contemporary poetry, remember that the modern poet has a lot to contend with:

Inspiration and genius
Are not everything.
While Shakespeare wrote
The telephone didn't ring.

# S HREWD SIMON SHORT

"Greek grapes", "Knapsack strap" and "Red leather, yellow leather" are three phrases that are barely repeatable. Pick one and rattle it off a dozen times in quick succession. Not easy, is it?

*The Guinness Book of Records* suggests that this might be the English language's trickiest tongue-twister: "The sixth sick sheik's sixth sheep's sick". It's fairly fiendish, but for me it pales into insignificance when set beside what I reckon has to be the world's worst – and longest – tongue-twister: "The Saga of Shrewd Simon Short".

Try to read it out loud without making a single slip. I couldn't do it. Can you?

Shrewd Simon Short sewed shoes. Seventeen summers, speeding storms, spreading sunshine successively, saw Simon's small, shabby shop, still standing staunch, saw Simon's selfsame squeaking sign still swinging silently specifying:

Simon Short, Smithfield's sole surviving shoemaker. Shoes sewed soled superfinely.

Simon's spry, sedulous spouse, Sally Short, sewed shirts,

stitched sheets, stuffed sofas. Simon's six stout sons – Seth, Samuel, Stephen, Saul, Silas, Shadrach – sold sundries. Sober Seth sold sugar, spices; simple Sam sold saddles, stirrups, screws; sagacious Stephen sold silks, satins, shawls; skeptical Saul sold silver salvers; selfish Shadrach sold salves, shoe-strings, soap, saws, skates; slack Silas sold Sally Short's stuffed sofas.

Some seven summers since, Simon's second son Samuel saw Sophia Sophronia Spriggs somewhere. Sweet, smart, sensible Sophia Sophronia Spriggs. Sam soon showed strong symptoms. Sam seldom stayed storing, selling saddles. Sam sighed sorrowfully, sought Sophia Sophronia's society, sung several serenades slyly. Simon stormed, scolded severely, said Sam seemed so silly singing such shameful, senseless songs. "Strange Sam should slight such splendid sales! Strutting spendthrift! Shattered-brained simpleton."

"Softly, softly, sire," said Sally. "Sam's smitten; Sam's spied some sweetheart."

"Sentimental schoolboy!" snarled Simon. "Smitten! Stop such stuff." Simon sent Sally's snuffbox spinning, seized Sally's scissors, smashed Sally's spectacles, scattering several* spools. "Sneaking scoundrel! Sam's shocking silliness shall surcease!" Scowling, Simon stopped speaking, started swiftly shopward. Sally sighed sadly. Summoning Sam, she spoke sweet sympathy. "Sam," said she, "sire seems singularly snappy; so, solicit, sue, secure Sophronia speedily, Sam."

"So soon? So soon?" said Sam, standing stock-still.

"So soon, surely," said Sally smiling, "specially since sire shows such spirits."

So Sam, somewhat scared, sauntered slowly, shaking stupendously, Sam soliloquizes: "Sophia Sophronia Spriggs, Spriggs – Short – Sophia Sophronia Short – Samuel Short's spouse – sounds splendid! Suppose she should say – she shan't – she shan't!"

Soon Sam spied Sophia starching shirts, singing softly. Seeing Sam she stopped starching, saluting Sam smilingly. Sam stammered shockingly.

"Spl-spl-splendid summer season, Sophia."

"Selling saddles still, Sam?"

"Sar-sar-tin," said Sam, starting suddenly. "Season's somewhat sudorific," said Sam, steadily, staunching streaming sweat, shaking sensibly.

"Sartin," said Sophia, smiling significantly. "Sip some sweet sherbet, Sam." (Silence sixty seconds.)

"Sire shot sixty sheldrakes, Saturday," said Sophia.

"Sixty? Sho!" said Sam. (Silence seventy-seven seconds.)

"See sister Susan's sunflowers," said Sophia socially, silencing such stiff silence.

Sophia's sprightly sauciness stimulated Sam strangely: so Sam suddenly spoke sentimentally: "Sophia, Susan's sunflowers seem saying Samuel Short, Sophia Sophronia Spriggs, stroll serenely, seek some sequestered spot, some sylvan shade. Sparkling springs shall sing soul-stirring strains; sweet songsters shall silence secret sighings; super-angelic sylphs shall" – Sophia snickered; so Sam stopped.

"Sophia," said Sam solemnly.

"Sam," said Sophia.

"Sophia, stop smiling; Sam Short's sincere. Sam's seeking some sweet spouse, Sophia."

Sophia stood silent.

"Speak, Sophia, speak; such suspense speculates sorrow."

"Seek, sire, Sam, seek sire."

So Sam sought sire Spriggs; sire Sprigs said, "Sartin."

P.S. If a Hottentot tot taught a Hottentot tot to talk e'er the tot could totter, ought the Hottentot tot be taught to say aught, or naught, or what ought to be taught her?

If to hoot and to toot a Hottentot tot be taught by a Hottentot tutor, should the tutor get hot if the Hottentot tot hoot and toot at the Hottentot tutor?

# R ULES OF THE GAME

A wise American recently observed: "The Lord's Prayer has 56 words; at Gettysburg, Lincoln spoke only 268 long-remembered words; and we got a whole country goin' on the 1,322 words in the Declaration of Independence. So how come it took the government 26,911 words to issue a regulation on the sale of cabbages?"

I don't know the answer to that one, but I do know that we would all write and speak better, clearer, and more understandable English if only we had learned the rules of the game. Which rules, you ask? These rules, say I:

1 Don't use no double negatives.

2 Make each pronoun agree with their antecedent.

3 Join clauses good, like a conjunction should.

4 About them sentence fragments.

5  When dangling watch your particles.

6  Verbs has to agree with their subjects.

7  Just between you and I, case is important too.

8  Don't write run-on sentences they are hard to read.

9  Don't use commas, which aren't necessary.

10  Try not to oversplit infinitives.

11  It is important to use your apostrophe's correctly.

12  Proofread your writing to if any words out.

13  Correct spelling is esential.

And here are two extra rules that, as a writer, I have found invaluable.

*The Oxford Rule.* It's is not, it isn't ain't, and it's it's, not its, if you mean it is. If you don't, it's its. Then too, it's hers. It isn't her's. It isn't our's either. It's ours, and likewise yours and theirs.

*Smith's Writing Rule.* In composing, as a general rule, run your pen through every word you have written; you have no idea what vigour it will give your style.

## LIFELAWS

I received a startling letter from a total stranger the other day. Let me quote it in full: "Dear Gyles, You seem to think you know a lot. Tell me, what is the meaning of life?"

Well, I don't like admitting this—and you may find it hard to believe—but I know almost nothing about the Meaning of Life. At the same time, I hate disappointing anyone; so, just for the fun of it, I gathered together a selection of Lifelaws—the rules, observations and maxims that may not explain *all* the mysteries of life on this planet but at least contribute something towards a better understanding of our earthly existence. Here they are:

*Blick's Rule of Life.* You have two chances, slim and non-existent.

*Brenne's Laws of Life.* (1) You never get it where you want it. (2) If you think it's tough now, just wait.

*Gandhi's Observation.* There is more to life than increasing its speed.

*Hovanick's Wait-till-Tomorrow Principle.* Today is the last day of the first part of your life.

*Howe's Verities.* (1) When you're in trouble, people who call to sympathize are really looking for the particulars. (2) When in doubt in society, shake hands. (3) Everyone hates a martyr; it's no wonder martyrs are burned at the stake. (4) A good many of your tragedies probably look like comedies to others. (5) Put cream and sugar on a fly, and it tastes very much like a black raspberry. (6) Families with babies and families without babies are sorry for each other. (7) Where the guests at a gathering are acquainted, they eat 20 per cent more than they otherwise would.

*Freud's Observation.* Shunning women, drink, gambling, smoking, and eating will not make one live longer; it will only seem like it.

*Lee's Law.* Mother said there would be days like this, but she never said there would be so many.

*Lichtenberg's Insights.* (1) If life were "just a bowl of cherries" ... we would soon die of a deficiency disease. (2) We can never get to the Promised Land, for if we did, it would no longer be the Promised Land. (3) We say that the plough made civilization, but for that matter, so did manure. (4) The planning laws in most American neighbourhoods would not *permit* the construction of a Parthenon.

*Lucy's Law.* The alternative to getting old is depressing.

*Paige's Six Rules of Life* (guaranteed to bring anyone to a happy old age). (1) Avoid fried foods that angry up the blood. (2) If your stomach antagonizes you, pacify it with cool thoughts. (3) Keep the juices flowing by jangling around gently as you move. (4) Go very lightly on the vices, such as carrying on in society, as the social ramble ain't restful. (5) Avoid running at all times. (6) Don't look back, something might be gaining on you.

*Quality-of-Life Constant.* Every time in your life when you think you are about to be able to make both ends meet, somebody moves the ends.

*Schwartz's True View of Life.* Don't look for your real success until you're past fifty. It takes that long to get over the distractions of sex.

*Schwartz's Maxim.* Live every day as if it were your last ... and some day you'll be right.

## SIGNS OF MATURITY

Or: How to know when you are growing older.

1 Everything hurts, and what doesn't hurt doesn't work.

2 The gleam in your eye is from the sun hitting your bifocals.

3 You feel like the night before, and you haven't been anywhere.

4 Your little black book contains only names ending in M.D.

5 You get winded playing chess.

6 Your children begin to look middle aged.

7 A dripping tap causes an uncontrollable bladder urge.

8 You join a health club and don't go.

9 You know all the answers, but nobody asks you the questions.

10 You look forward to a dull evening.

11 You turn out the lights for economic rather than romantic reasons.

12 You sit in a rocking chair and can't get it going.

13 Your knees buckle but your belt won't.

14 Your back goes out more than you do.

15 The little grey-haired lady you help across the street is your wife.

16 You have too much room in the house and not enough in the medicine cabinet.

17 You sink your teeth into a steak, and they stay there.

# QUOTE UNQUOTE

Messing about in quotes is one of my favourite pastimes, and many of my favourite quotes have to do with words and language. Of my favourites the twenty-five that follow are my most favourite. (*Favourite*, incidentally, is one of my favourite words. I hope you don't think I overuse it. I try to avoid clichés like the plague.)

Man is a creature who lives not upon bread alone, but principally by catchwords. (ROBERT LOUIS STEVENSON)

Man does not live by words alone, despite the fact that sometimes he has to eat them. (ADLAI STEVENSON)

Words, in their primary or immediate signification, stand for nothing but the ideas in the mind of him who uses them. (JOHN LOCKE)

If language be not in accordance with the truth of things, affairs cannot be carried on to success. (CONFUCIUS)

If a people have no word for something, either it does not matter to them or it matters too much to talk about it. (EDGAR Z. FRIEDENBERG)

Words should be an intense pleasure just as leather should be to a shoemaker. (EVELYN WAUGH)

Neither is a dictionary a bad book to read. There is no cant in it, no excess of explanation, and it is full of suggestion – the raw material of possible poems and histories. (RALPH WALDO EMERSON)

Dictionaries are like watches: the worst is better than none, and the best cannot be expected to go quite true. (SAMUEL JOHNSON)

When I feel inclined to read poetry I take down my dictionary. The poetry of words is quite as beautiful as that of sentences. (OLIVER WENDELL HOLMES, SR.)

The trouble with the dictionary is that you have to know how a word is spelled before you can look it up to see how it is spelled. (WILL CUPPY)

Many people would be more truthful were it not for their uncontrollable desire to talk. (EDWARD WATSON HOWE)

Talkers are no good doers. (WILLIAM SHAKESPEARE)

The habit of common and continuous speech is a symptom of mental deficiency. It proceeds from not knowing what is going on in other people's minds. (WALTER BAGEHOT)

Learned conversation is either the affectation of the ignorant or the profession of the mentally unemployed. (OSCAR WILDE)

The art of conversation is the art of hearing as well as of being heard. (WILLIAM HAZLITT)

It usually takes more than three weeks to prepare a good impromptu speech. (MARK TWAIN)

An unusual word should be shunned as a ship would shun a reef. (JULIUS CAESAR)

Short words are best and the old words when short are best of all. (WINSTON CHURCHILL)

Actions lie louder than words. (CAROLYN WELLS)

The Romans would never have found time to conquer the world if they had been obliged first to learn Latin. (HEINRICH HEINE)

A man of words and not deeds is like a garden full of weeds. (ENGLISH PROVERB)

A fine quotation is a diamond on the finger of a man of wit, and a pebble in the hand of a fool. (JOSEPH ROUX)

A short saying oft contains much wisdom. (SOPHOCLES)

I hate quotations. Tell me what you know. (RALPH WALDO EMERSON)

## WHAT I KNOW

I know I love quotations, especially ones that make you smile – and think, like these:

If the art of conversation stood a little higher, we would have a lower birthrate. (STANISLAW LEC)

Bureaucracy is based on a willingness either to pass the buck or spend it. (MRS. HENRY J. SERWAT)

It's hard to know exactly when one generation ends and the next one begins. But it's somewhere around nine o'clock at night. (CHARLES RUFFING)

My interest is in the future, because I am going to spend the rest of my life there. (CHARLES KETTERING)

EROS: spelled backwards gives you an idea of how it affects beginners. (ANONYMOUS)

To double your salary, Xerox your paycheck. (PAT O'HAIRE)

If soldiers were asked to do in battle what the average motorist does on weekends for fun, the officer in charge would be court-martialled for brutality. (MALCOLM MUGGERIDGE

When in doubt, tell the truth. (MARK TWAIN)

A kiss that speaks volumes is seldom a first edition. (CLARE WHITING)

Whenever you hear the word *save*, it is usually the beginning of an advertisement designed to make you spend money. (RENÉE PIERRE-GOSSET)

If God had meant people to go nude, they would have been born that way.

If God had meant us to go metric, why did He give Christ twelve apostles?

# Pray time

How long (O Lord) will it be, I wonder, before our prayers have been translated into the language of our times? The jargoneers are working on the Psalms already: "The Lord and I are in a shepherd/sheep situation and I am in a position of negative need . . ."

With a little luck – and possibly some divine intervention – the language of prayer may remain sacred for a few years yet.

It's the *language* of prayer that is so compelling, even if some of the *sentiments* expressed are not so worthy.

### THE PARLIAMENTARY PRAYER

Yea, though I graze in pastures with jackasses,
I pray that I may not bray like one.

## THE BIGOT'S PRAYER

Grant, O God, that we may always be right, for Thou knowest we will
never change our minds.

## THE FISHERMAN'S PRAYER

Give me, O Lord, to catch a fish
    So large that even I,
In boasting of it afterwards,
    Shall have no need to lie.

## THE PRAGMATIST'S PRAYER

Searcher of souls, You who in heaven abide,
To whom the secrets of all hearts are open,
Though I do lie to all the word beside,
From me to Thee no falsehoods shall be spoken.
Cleanse me not, Lord, I say, from secret sin
But from those faults which he who runs can see.
'Tis these that torture me, O Lord, begin
With these and let the hidden vices be;
If You must cleanse these too, at any rate
Deal with the seen sins first, 'tis only reason,
They being so gross, to let the others wait
The leisure of some more convenient season;
    And cleanse not all even then, leave me a few,
    I would not be – not quite – so pure as You.

## PRAYER OF A POOR PEDESTRIAN

O God, who filled all heaven with stars
And then all earth with motorcars,
    Make room within thy cosmic plan
    For me, a poor pedestrian.

Spread Thou before me, I entreat,
A threadlike pathway for my feet;
    And do Thou watch me lest I stray
    From this, Thy strait and narrow way.

Give me an ear alert, acute,
For each swift car's peremptory hoot:
    Teach me to judge its headlong pace
    And dodge it with a nimble grace.

When drivers' looks and words are black,
Restrain me, Lord, from answering back:
    O bless me with a nature meek
    To bear with smiles each narrow squeak.

And if one day Thy watchful eye
Should be withdrawn, and I should die,
    One boon I crave, upon my knees:
    Exonerate the driver, please.

## THE VENDOR'S PRAYER

On Sunday, Lord, a Mrs Drew
Is coming here the house to view,
    Which is, of course, for sale.
Grant Thou, O Lord, that she forbear
From standing long upon the stair
    That is, alas! too frail.

O do not let her hand draw back
The curtain and reveal the crack
    Along the windowpane!
O guide her as she comes and goes,
So that no smell assails her nose
    From the adjacent drain.

Let her not see the neighbouring slum
As she approaches. May she come
    Along the better road,
And grant that she may, in a trice,
Agree to the inflated price
    We ask for our abode.

And grant, O Lord, to us who plead,
These favours that we may succeed
    In what we now devise,
And through Thine all-embracing love
Be made eternal tenants of
    Thy mansion in the skies.

## THE HUSBAND'S PRAYER

Lord, on whom all love depends,
Let me make and keep good friends:

Bless me, also, with the patience
To endure my wife's relations.


## THE BARGAINING PRAYER

Lord, give us grace, for if Thou give us not grace, we shall not
give Thee glory; and who will win by that, Lord?

## NOT A PRAYER

Recently a prayer – albeit not a very poetic one – managed to
make legal history when it was quoted in the trial of a man
accused of starting a forest fire in British Columbia.

The accused claimed that what he had said was
inadmissible as evidence because it formed part of a "private
conversation" he was having with God. The judge ruled that it
was not possible to have a genuine conversation with God since
He/She was not legally a person.

Consequently the man's prayer was admitted as evidence
and established as proof of his guilt. This was the unfortunate
prayer: "Oh God, please let me get away with it, just this once."

# OH NO IT'S NOT!

The world of words is full of surprises. You might think that a *barguest* is a guest in a bar, but, oh no, it's not. It's a ghost or a goblin, often shaped like a large dog. If you need further proof that words aren't always what they seem, here it is:

> *Bedrape* is not rape occurring in a bed; but is an intensive form of the verb *drape*.
>
> *Bedrug* is not a bedspread; but is an intensive form of the verb *drug*.
>
> *Carlot* is not a place for parking or displaying cars; but is an obsolete term for a book.
>
> *Deadlily* is not a dead lily; but is an adverb meaning "in a deadly manner".
>
> *Forestation* is not a station or outpost at a frontier; but is the establishment of a forest.
>
> *Forestress* is not a female forester; but is a verb meaning "to place stress on the first part of a word".

*Interminable* is not an adjective meaning "to penetrate with mines"; but is an adjective meaning "long-lasting".

*Intermine* is not a verb meaning "to last for a long time"; but is a verb meaning "to penetrate with mines".

*Negrocop* is not a black policeman; but is a type of stork, also called the jabiru.

*Nunlet* is not a small nun; but is a small South American bird.

*Racemate* is not a member of the same race; but is a chemical salt of racemic acid.

*Redial* is not a verb meaning "to dial again"; but is an adjective meaning "relating to redia, a type of larva".

*Restable* is not a verb meaning "to stable again"; but is an adjective meaning "able to rest".

*Sealess* is not a female seal; but is an adjective meaning "without a sea".

*Tonite* is not only a slang spelling of *tonight*; but is also a blasting explosive.

*Townsite* is not a mineral named after someone named Towns; but is the site of a town.

*Wellsite* is not the site of a well; but is a mineral named after someone named Wells.

# N EOLOGISTS AT WORK

In the 1960s, '70s, and '80s, the neologists have been hard at work, creating brand-new words for a brave new world. Here are thirty long ones:

antientertainment

biodeterioration

biogeocoenology

bourgeoisification

comprehensivization

containershipping

counterdemonstrator

cross-subsidization

dendroclimatologist

electrogasdynamic

embourgeoisification

encephalomyocarditis

Finlandization

hyperlipoproteinemia

intergenerational

Malaysianization

Manhattanization

megahallucinogen

microearthquake

mini-black-hole

neuropharmacological
nucleocosmochronology
pachycephalosaurian
psychedelicatessen
psychobiographical

suggestopaedia
tephrochronological
transhistorical
undercharacterization
Washingtonologist

And here are thirty phrases of our time. Each has made its way into the dictionary during the final third of the twentieth century:

animal lib
big enchilada
brown power
clockwork orange
double nickel
empty nest syndrome
floppy disk
game plan
home computer
hot pants
incomes policy
Jesus freak
junk food
kinky boot
last hurrah

male chauvinist piggery
meter maid
neutron bomb
oil spill
phone phreakdom
quick and dirty
reverse discrimination
Saturday night special
tadpole galaxy
urban sprawl
value-added tax
Wankel engine
X-rated
youth culture
zero population growth

## BARNHART LANGUAGE

*A Dictionary of New English* and *The Second Barnhart Dictionary of New English*, both by Clarence Barnhart, Robert Barnhart, and Sol Steinmetz, were published in 1973 and 1980, respectively, and they feature words, initials, phrases, abbreviations, acronyms, and meanings that have entered the vocabulary of the English language in very recent years.

A number of the entries are of words relating to words. Here are thirty:

| | |
|---|---|
| *acrolect* | The dialect that has the most prestige among the speakers of a language. |
| *AmeroEnglish* | American English. |
| *bookaholic* | A person addicted to books. |
| *businesspeak* | Commercial jargon. |
| *dead letter box* | A place for depositing secret messages. |
| *educationese* | Jargon used by people associated with education. |
| *encryption* | The act of putting information into a code. |
| *English English* | English as spoken in England. |
| *Englishment* | An English version of a foreign work. |
| *exonym* | Any of the names given in different countries or languages to the same geographical feature. |
| *expletive deleted* | An expression indicating the omission from print of an obscene word or phrase. |
| *factoid* | A published statement taken to be a fact by virtue of its appearance in print. |
| *familygram* | A brief radio message transmitted by relatives to a sailor at sea. |
| *francisize* | To cause to change to the French language. |
| *francophonic* | French-speaking. |
| *franglification* | The introduction of English words and expressions into French. |
| *Fringlish* | English containing French words and expressions. |
| *Hinglish* | A blend of Hindi and English spoken in India. |
| *Japlish* | A blend of Japanese and English spoken in Japan. |
| *jargonaut* | A person who uses jargon excessively. |
| *Jonah word* | Any word that a chronic stutterer has difficulty uttering in ordinary conversation. |

| | |
|---|---|
| *lansign* | A word, character, or sound that represents a thing or idea. |
| *pangram* | A sentence made up to include all the letters of the alphabet. |
| *psychobabble* | Psychological jargon. |
| *semiliterate* | A person barely able to read and write. |
| *single-entendre* | A word, expression, or statement with an unmistakable and often indelicate meaning. |
| *Spanglish* | A blend of Spanish and English spoken in parts of the western United States and Latin America. |
| *whydunit* | A mystery novel that deals primarily with the motivation for the crime. |
| *wordaholic* | A word addict. |
| *Yinglish* | English containing many Yiddish words and expressions. |

## TIMELY NEOLOGISMS

For well over four decades now, *Time* magazine has been introducing words to the English language.

*Tycoon, kudos, pundit,* and *socialite* all gained currency from their use in *Time*. The magazine was the first to put *Op* in *Op Art*, and it led the way in popularizing scores of new words, from *GI* to *A-Bomb*, from *beatnik* to *McCarthyism*, and from *Kremlinologist* to *Sinologist*. Of course *Time* has had its share of failures. It tried hard with *cinemactor, cinemactress,* and *cinemogul,* but none of them caught on.

Here are some of *Time*'s new words from the sixties and seventies. The magazine created many of the words and popularized the others. What all the words have in common is that when *Time* was first published none of them existed.

| | |
|---|---|
| amorific (1975) | apocalypticians (1972) |
| anti-opera (1968) | audioanimatronically (1973) |
| anti-star (1969) | Beatledammerung (1971) |

bewilderness (1973)

biographoid (1973)

blaxploitation (1974)

buffdom (1974)

Californicated (1971)

Carterphobia (1976)

cavepersons (1976)

chillout (1973)

counterklutzical (1976)

crediholics (1977)

culturecrats (1970)

Disneyfication (1977)

eco-activists (1969)

ejaculatorium (1972)

girlcott (1970)

growthmania (1977)

heightism (1971)

hippophile (1970)

horsepersons (1976)

jivernacular (1975)

lumpengrandiosity (1974)

mailgrams (1977)

Maocidal (1977)

mathemagician (1977)

mazemania (1975)

megabuckers (1977)

megadisaster (1976)

Msapprehension (1972)

Msogamy (1971)

occultivated (1975)

oligosyllabic (1971)

orgasmatron (1975)

outcumbent (1976)

paperkrieg (1973)

parafictions (1977)

petroglitter (1975)

petropolitics (1973)

phallocrat (1977)

philodendrophiles (1974)

plantochondriacs (1974)

polycopulative (1971)

prognosticide (1974)

radicalesbians (1970)

roadies (1973)

schleprechaun (1972)

sci-fireworks (1976)

sexscraper (1970)

sociohysteric (1973)

space-bopper (1975)

superbug (1977)

supercrooner (1973)

superpregnancy (1973)

superscapegoat (1973)

systemaniac (1977)

televangelist (1973)

UFOria (1976)

underworldly (1970)

unsavvy (1976)

urbanscape (1975)

verballistics (1972)

vestphobe (1974)

watch-birds (1971)

womandarin (1972)

wommanequin (1971)

womlibby (1973)

## MEDICINEOLOGY

Of course, living in the 1980s we all face certain health hazards. Fortunately, the neologists among the medics have found appropriate names for the ailments of our times. These ten were noted by *The New England Journal of Medicine*:

Rubik Cuber's Tendonitis

Yo-Yoers Finger

Jogger's Nipple

Cyclist's Pudendum

Dog Walker's Elbow

Space Invader's Wrist

Unicyclist's Sciatica

Jeans Folliculitis

Flautist's Neuropathy

Urban Cowboy's Rhabdomyolisis (A muscular pain caused by riding mechanical bucking broncos in amusement arcades.)

In the City in 1987 a new and deadly peril came to light: A.I.D.S – the Addictive Insider Dealing Syndrome.

# Making a Name in the States

In *Webster's Third New International Dictionary*, the noun *Chicago* is defined as a method of playing contract bridge in sets of four deals rather than rubbers. The dictionary also indicates that *Chicago* is a synonym for *Michigan*, a type of card game. I wonder just how many people know that *Chicago* and *Michigan* are one and the same thing?

It's surprising how many American city names happen to have alternative meanings. Take these for a start:

| | |
|---|---|
| *Amarillo* | A Venezuelan tree. |
| *Atlanta* | A genus of molluscs. |
| *Austin* | Relating to St. Augustus. |
| *Baltimore* | A butterfly. |
| *Boston* | A waltz. |

| | |
|---|---|
| *Buffalo* | To bewilder. |
| *Charlotte* | A dessert. |
| *Cincinnati* | A wild-card poker game. |
| *Dearborn* | A light four-wheeled carriage. |
| *Denver* | Battleship grey, a colour. |
| *Fresno* | A modified drag scraper, an earth digging device. |
| *Long Beach* | A light yellowish brown colour. |
| *Milwaukee* | A variety of apple. |
| *Montgomery* | An Asian Indian breed of dairy cattle. |
| *Phoenix* | A legendary bird. |
| *Springfield* | A US army rifle. |
| *Toledo* | A sword. |
| *Wichita* | An Indian people. |
| *Worcester* | A type of china or porcelain. |
| *Yonkers* | Young men. |

Some US state names have unexpected alternative meanings too. Look at these:

| | |
|---|---|
| *Alabama* | A genus of moths. |
| *Alaska* | A mixed yarn. |
| *Arkansas* | A type of apple. |
| *Delaware* | One of a breed of fowls. |
| *Florida* | A large yellow peach. |
| *Georgia* | A feminine proper name. |
| *Idaho* | A potato. |
| *Indiana* | A vivid red colour. |
| *Kansas* | An adjective used to refer to the second glacial stage during the glacial epoch in North America. |
| *Maine* | To lower a sail. |
| *Maryland* | Tobacco. |
| *Michigan* | A card game. |
| *Minnesota* | A breed of swine. |
| *Mississippi* | A game resembling bagatelle. |

| | |
|---|---|
| *Montana* | A sheep. |
| *Nevada* | Pseudonymous surname of Emma Wixom, an American singer. |
| *New Hampshire* | A fowl. |
| *Oklahoma* | A form of gin rummy. |
| *Oregon* | A ship. |
| *Texas* | The narrow topmost story of a grain elevator. |

## CHICAGO

Everyone is familiar with the name Chicago, but the way we spell it today isn't how it has always been spelled. In fact there is probably no other city in the United States whose name over the years has been spelled in so many different ways. *Chicago* is a word of Indian origin, supposedly meaning "garlic", "wild onion" and "skunk".

Can you guess how many known alternative spellings for *Chicago* there have been over the past three hundred years?

(See Answers, page 260.)

## DING DONG IN TEXAS

The United States boasts some remarkable place names. I've made a list of some of the oddest. They may seem incredible, but you'll find every one of them on the map.

| | |
|---|---|
| Aaat's Bay | (Alaska) |
| Bad Axe | (Michigan) |
| Battiest | (Oklahoma) |
| Bald Knob | (Arkansas) |
| Bird in Hand | (Pennsylvania) |
| Blue Earth | (Minnesota) |
| Broken Bow | (Nebraska) |
| Bug | (Kentucky) |
| Cut Off | (Louisiana) |

| | |
|---|---|
| Cut and Shoot | (Texas) |
| Ding Dong | (Texas) |
| D'Lo | (Mississippi) |
| E | (Maine) |
| Eek | (Alaska) |
| Eighty Eight | (Kentucky) |
| Embarrass | (Wisconsin) |
| Enigma | (Georgia) |
| Flying H | (New Mexico) |
| Gravel Switch | (Kentucky) |
| Gu Vo | (Arizona) |
| Hi Hat | (Kentucky) |
| Horse Thief | (Arizona) |
| Hungry Horse | (Montana) |
| Intercourse | (Pennsylvania) |
| Jackass Flats | (Nevada) |
| King of Prussia | (Pennsylvania) |
| Kupk | (Arizona) |
| Left Hand | (West Virginia) |
| Marrowbone | (Kentucky) |
| Mexican Hat | (Utah) |
| Nameless | (Kentucky) |
| Novelty | (Ohio) |
| Only | (Tennessee) |
| Plain Dealing | (Louisiana) |
| Sikul Himatk | (Arizona) |
| Sivili Chuchg | (Arizona) |
| Slap Out | (Illinois) |
| Smoky Ordinary | (Virginia) |
| Social Circle | (Georgia) |
| Sweet Gum Head | (Louisiana) |
| Tobacco | (Kentucky) |
| Truth or Consequences | (New Mexico) |
| Uncle Same | (Louisiana) |

| | |
|---|---|
| Wawk Hudunk | (Arizona) |
| What Cheer | (Iowa) |
| Why | (Arizona) |
| Whynot | (Mississippi) |
| Wounded Knee | (South Dakota) |
| Yum Yum | (Tennessee) |
| Zzyzx Springs | (California) |

## WYOMING IN DELAWARE

My good friend Darryl Francis, committed verbivore and student of geography, has discovered that there are two hundred cities, towns, and communities in the United States that have names that happen also to be the names of states. For example, there is a town called *Oregon* in Holt County, Missouri, and a *Maine* in Davie County, North Carolina.

There is even a *New Hampshire* in Auglaize County, Ohio, and a *West Virginia* in St. Louis County, Minnesota.

Here are twenty-six of the places Darryl discovered, arranged in an elegant chain of town and state names:

*Wyoming* is in Kent County, Delaware.

*Delaware* is in Southampton County, Virginia.

*Virginia* is in Kitsap County, Washington.

*Washington* is in Knox County, Maine.

*Maine* is in Coconino County, Arizona.

*Arizona* is in Burt County, Nebraska.

*Nebraska* is in Jennings County, Indiana.

*Indiana* is in Indiana County, Pennsylvania.

*Pennsylvania* is in Mobile County, Alabama.

*Alabama* is in Genesee County, New York.

*New York* is in Santa Rosa County, Florida.

*Florida* is in Houghton County, Michigan.

*Michigan* is in Osage County, Kansas.

*Kansas* is in Seneca County, Ohio.

*Ohio* is in Gunnison County, Colorado.

*Colorado* is in South Central District, Alaska.

*Alaska* is in Mineral County, West Virginia.

*West Virginia* is in St. Louis County, Minnesota.

*Minnesota* is in Colquitt County, Georgia.

*Georgia* is in Lamar County, Texas.

*Texas* is in Baltimore County, Maryland.

*Maryland* is in East Baton Rouge County, Louisiana.

*Louisiana* is in Pike County, Missouri.

*Missouri* is in Brown County, Illinois.

*Illinois* is in Sequoyah County, Oklahoma.

*Oklahoma* is in Daviess County, Kentucky.

## I'M ACHING FOR MICHIGAN

Rearrange the letters in *Colorado*, and you can make *coal odor* or *cool road*. Rearrange the letters in the names of two dozen other states, and you get a curious collection of alternative words, names, and places.

| | |
|---|---|
| *Alaska* | *Akalas* are certain shrubs that bear large red edible fruits and come from the Hawaiian Islands. |
| *Arizona* | *Arzonia* is a girl's given name; *Azorian* is a native of the Azores Islands; *Zonaria* is a group of mammals including the carnivores and certain ungulates. |
| *Arkansas* | *Sankara's* is the possessive or genitive form of Sankara, a famous Hindu philosopher who flourished around A.D. 800. *Sanskara* is a Hindu ceremony that purifies the taint of sin contracted in the womb. |
| *California* | *African oil* is a type of palm oil yielded by a tall palm tree, the African oil palm. |
| *Delaware* | *Aleeward* is toward the sheltered side; *Weardale* is a district of the town of Durham in England. |

| | |
|---|---|
| *Florida* | *Forlaid* is the past tense of *forlay*, to hinder or obstruct. |
| *Idaho* | *Adhoi* is a town in India, west of Ahmedabad, along the Tropic of Cancer. |
| *Illinois* | *Illision* is the act of dashing or striking against something. |
| *Indiana* | *Anidian* is an adjective meaning "formless" or "without shape". |
| *Iowa* | *Aiwo* is one of the fourteen regions of Nauru Island, in the Pacific; *Awio* Bay is on the southern coast of New Britain, in New Guinea. |
| *Kansas* | *Asansk* is a town northeast of Krasnoyarsk, in west central Siberia; *Kassan* is a town southwest of Samarkand in Uzbekistan; *Nassak* is the name of a world-famous diamond. (Note that *Kassan* and *Nassak* are reversals of each other.) |
| *Maine* | *Amine* is a type of organic compound; *Meina* is a town in Italy; *Menai* Strait is in Wales; *Namie* is a town in Japan. |
| *Maryland* | *Marlandy* Hill is a 1,230-foot-high hill near the western coast of Australia. |
| *Minnesota* | *Mainstone* is a town in Shropshire, England; *mannitose* is a type of sugar; *nominates* simply means "designates". |
| *Montana* | *Manaton* is a town in Devon, England. |
| *Nebraska* | *Bankeras* are stone curlews of Santo Domingo; *Branksea* is an ecclesiastical district in southeast Devon, England. |
| *Nevada* | *Adaven* is a community in Nye County, Nevada. (Note that this is *Nevada* spelled backwards.) *Venada* is another name for a pudu, a type of deer. |
| *New York* | *Ywroken* is an old form of the past participle of the verb *wreak*, now occupied by *wrought*. |
| *Ohio* | *Hooi* is the sound made by the wind whistling around a corner or through a keyhole. |

| Oregon | *Orgone* is a vital energy held to pervade nature and to be accumulable, in a specially designed box, for use by humans; *oronge* is an old spelling of *orange*. |
| Texas | *Sexta* is a feminine first name; *taxes* is the plural of *tax*. |
| Utah | *Ahut* is a fourteenth-century variant spelling of *aught*; *haut* is an old word for *height*; *thau* is the twenty-third letter of the Hebrew alphabet, also called *tav* and *taw*. |
| Virginia | *Irvingia* is a genus of tree. |
| Washington | *Nowanights* is the night-time equivalent of nowadays. |

## TEEN SENSE IN TENNESSEE

Take these twenty words and rearrange the letters in each word to form the names of twenty American cities.

| | | | |
|---|---|---|---|
| 1 | annotations | 11 | Havanans |
| 2 | brogan* | 12 | hounds |
| 3 | capers | 13 | long leases |
| 4 | caption | 14 | meals |
| 5 | counts | 15 | nerved |
| 6 | diagnose | 16 | ordeal |
| 7 | domains | 17 | Nero |
| 8 | dottier | 18 | salvages |
| 9 | emendator | 19 | tooled |
| 10 | grained* | 20 | wine cellars |

(See Answers, page 260.)

*You can find these two in Britain as well.

# L ARGESSE IS A CAPITAL S

These aren't genuine howlers. They are bogus bloopers made up by those who know better but want to raise a smile.

1 *Largesse* is a capital *S*.

2 A male escort is known as a *mandate*.

3 *Maritime affairs* refer to what happens on wedding days.

4 Judges always appear in a *lawsuit*.

5 *Cereal* is an adjective that describes the painting style of Salvador Dali.

6 A *bombard* is a lousy poet.

7 A *locomotion* is a faint noise.

8 A *handicap* is a ready hat.

9 Your ex-spouse is known as a *stalemate*.

10 A *shamrock* is a fake diamond.

These ones are the real thing: genuine mistakes committed by the innocent in schools and colleges around the English-speaking world.

1 Flaura and Fauna were the original Siamese twins.

2 *A priori* means first come first served.

3 *Iran* is the Moslem Bible.

4 The eastern part of Asia is called Euthenasia.

5 *Mata Hari* means suicide in Japanese.

6 Poetic licence is the licence you need so that you can sell poetry.

7 Plenipotentiary is a place where foreign prisoners are kept.

8 The Merchant of Venice was a famous Italian who bought and sold canal boats.

9 Electric volts are named after Voltaire who discovered electricity.

10 When a woman has many husbands she is called a Pollyanna.

11 A stowaway is the man with the biggest appetite on the ship.

12 The Latin Quarter is a French twenty-five-cent piece.

Dr Alan Adell, Professor of Semantics at the University of Michigan in Ann Arbor, has recently completed a study of high-school vocabularies and come to the conclusion that children are much more likely to misunderstand a word if they hear it spoken than if they see it written. The students were each asked to define one hundred words given to them orally/aurally. These are some of the ones they got wrong.

| | |
|---|---|
| *adamant* | Pertaining to original sin. |
| *agnostics* | Behaviour of sound. |
| *allegro* | Chorus line |
| *amidst* | Thick fog. |
| *anthem* | Quite good-looking. |
| *antibody* | Diet. |
| *antimony* | Money inherited from an aunt. |
| *appendix* | Part of a book with little use. |
| *asperity* | Drug from which aspirins are made. |

| | |
|---|---|
| *aviary* | Pilots' dormitory. |
| *bibliography* | Holy geography. |
| *blizzard* | Inside of a chicken. |
| *buttress* | Nanny goat. |
| *caboose* | Indian baby. |
| *centimetre* | Insect with one hundred legs. |
| *chinchilla* | Icepack for lower half of the face. |
| *concubine* | Merger of several businesses. |
| *conservation* | Table talk. |
| *counterspy* | Store detective. |
| *dermatology* | Study of derms. |
| *deciduous* | Able to make up one's mind. |
| *diatribe* | Food for the whole clan. |
| *diva* | Swimming champion. |
| *effusive* | Able to be merged. |
| *epitaph* | Short, sarcastic poem. |
| *equestrian* | Person living on the equator. |
| *executive* | Man who puts others to death. |
| *finesse* | Female fish. |
| *firecracker* | Hot biscuit. |
| *genealogy* | Allergic to denim. |
| *gullible* | To do with sea birds. |
| *hackneyed* | Opposite of knock-kneed. |
| *hysterics* | Letters in sloping type. |
| *ingenious* | Not very smart. |
| *incommode* | Engaged, occupied. |
| *journeyman* | Travelling man. |
| *kilocycle* | Dangerous two-wheeler. |
| *longevity* | Being very tall. |
| *long-winded* | In good physical condition. |
| *nitrate* | Off-peak charges. |
| *optimists* | Doctors that treat your eyes. |
| *pedigree* | Teacher in college. |
| *pemmican* | Large bird with large bill. |

| | |
|---|---|
| *physics* | Different shapes of the human body. |
| *polyglot* | More than one glot. |
| *polygon* | Another name for a Mormon. |
| *preface* | Before applying makeup. |
| *reefs* | Objects placed on coffins. |
| *sabbatical year* | Year with fifty-three Sundays. |
| *semiquaver* | Half afraid. |
| *stalemate* | Husband or wife no longer interesting. |
| *telepathy* | Code invented by Morse. |
| *tenet* | Group of ten singers. |
| *typographer* | Student and drawer of maps. |
| *vicar* | Masculine form of *vixen*. |

# K.O. OK?

Told by a lady from Boston that her ancestors had sailed on the *Mayflower*, Will Rogers calmly replied that his ancestors had been waiting on the beach to meet them.

When you are bandying words with a true wit like Will Rogers, you'd better watch out. With his kind, you can find yourself K.O.'d before you realize the fight's begun.

I relish accounts of wits at work – and the more wicked and waspish they are in their wittiness the happier I am. From your ringside seat you should be able to relax and enjoy these fifteen rounds. After all, you can afford to. You're not one of the victims.

Ensnared by a fellow Bostonian who had pretensions to great piety, Mark Twain suffered the man for several minutes while he recounted his latest works of charity, concluding with the solemn pronouncement that his greatest ambition was to travel to the Holy Land and recite the Ten Commandments on Mt Sinai before he died.

"Really," said Twain, "and why not stay here in Boston and keep them?"

Only a few years before his death, Mozart was visited by a young composer who wanted to know how to write a symphony.

"You're very young," the great man told him. "Shouldn't you start by composing ballads?"

"But you were composing symphonies when you were only ten."

"I know," said Mozart, "but I didn't have to ask how."

In the first half of the nineteenth century Henry Clay was a major force in American politics and famous for his intolerance of the loquacious. Sitting in the Senate one day, he was forced to listen to one of the most prolix members of the House, who insisted on punctuating his speech with erudite references and rhetorical flourishes. Eventually Clay got to his feet and complained to the Speaker about the man.

"You, sir, speak for the present generation," said the aggrieved orator. "But I speak for posterity."

"Yes," replied Clay, "and you seem resolved to speak until the arrival of your audience."

During his term as Governor of New Jersey, Woodrow Wilson took a phone call informing him of the sudden death of one of his great friends, who represented the State in Congress. While he was still sitting at his desk, stunned by the news, the phone rang again. This time it was another New Jersey politician who had also heard the sad news but who wanted to capitalize on the sudden announcement. Could he take the deceased senator's place?

"Well, you may quote me as saying that's perfectly agreeable to me if it's agreeable to the undertaker," Wilson told him.

The journalist Heywood Broun was sent to interview a haughty politician on a controversial subject.

"I have nothing to say, young man," said the politico before Broun had even opened his notebook.

"I know," Broun told him. "Now, shall we get on with the interview?"

"Mr President, you must give me a colonel's commission for my son," a pushy mother informed Abraham Lincoln. "Sir, I demand it, not as a favour, but as a right. Sir, my grandfather fought at Lexington. Sir, my uncle was the only man who did not run away at Bladensburg. Sir, my father fought at New Orleans, and my husband was killed at Monterey."

"I guess, madam, your family has done enough for the country," Lincoln told her. "I think the time has come to give somebody else a chance."

Trying to capture the right expression from a very talkative and fidgety subject, Max Liebermann, the famous Berlin artist, silenced the woman with the comment:

"One more word out of you and I'll paint you as you are."

Once, when the artist William McNeill Whistler was in France and dining in a fashionable restaurant, he extended the hand of kindness and had it bitten. At the table next to him sat an Englishman who was experiencing some difficulty in placing an order in French.

"May I help you?" enquired Whistler politely, only to receive a curt rebuff to the effect that the man could manage on his own.

"I fancied contrary just now," replied Whistler, "when I heard you desire the waiter to bring you a pair of stairs."

Asked her opinion of a fellow artiste, the legendary Sarah Bernhardt replied:

"She's a wonderful actress from the waist down."

In the same (varicose) vein, Bette Davis is said to have remarked once of a Hollywood starlet: "There goes the good time that's had by all."

An amateur critic who buttonholed George S. Kaufman after one of his opening nights was taken aback by the author's rebuff when he ventured his opinion of the play.

"Perhaps you don't realize who I am?" said the man.

"That's only half of it," replied Kaufman.

Movie mogul Jed Harris had the disconcerting habit of occasionally greeting visitors stark naked. George S. Kaufman went to see him about the filming of one of his plays and brushed his full-frontal eccentricity aside by casually remarking: "Mr Harris, your fly is open."

"I want to thank you, Mr Marx, for all the enjoyment you've given the world," said a friendly old clergyman meeting Groucho for the first time.

"And I want to thank you for all the enjoyment you've taken out of it," replied Groucho.

The distinguished French writer Antoine de Rivarol was once asked his opinion of a couplet presented to him by an over-enthusiastic poet. After reading the two lines through several times, Rivarol handed them back to their author:

"Very nice, though there are dull stretches."

# J UST A LINE

> I may be the first albino transvestite to become President, but I'm not a murderer – am I?

That's the first line of my next novel, and I hope you like it because it's as far as I've got.

With a novel that hopes to become a classic or a best seller (and I want mine to be both), an arresting opening is essential. It may be just a line, but since it's got to grab the attention of the reader, it could claim to be the most important line in the book.

Here are the names of twenty successful novelists and the beguiling/intriguing/gripping opening sentences of twenty different novels. Can you decide who wrote what and give the title of each of the novels in question?

## TWENTY NOVELISTS

Frederick Forsyth
F. Scott Fitzgerald
Gustave Flaubert
Agatha Christie
Jean Paul Sartre
Daphne du Maurier
John Steinbeck
George Orwell
Robert M. Pirsig
Laurence Sterne

Graham Greene
Franz Kafka
Leo Tolstoy
Norman Mailer
Charles Dickens
Jack Kerouac
L. P. Hartley
Ernest Hemingway
Virginia Woolf
Kurt Vonnegut

## TWENTY NOVEL OPENINGS

1 Mr Tench went out to look for his ether cylinder into the blazing Mexican sun and the bleaching dust.

2 The best thing would be to write down everything that happens from day to day.

3 Life goes on, yes – and a fool and his self-respect are soon parted, perhaps never to be reunited even on Judgment Day.

4 When the east wind blows up the Helford river the shining waters are troubled and disturbed, and the little waves beat angrily upon the sandy shores.

5 Robert Cohn was once middleweight boxing champion of Princeton.

6 London. Michaelmas Term lately over, and the Lord Chancellor sitting in Lincoln's Inn Hall. Implacable November weather.

7 Someone must have been spreading lies about Joseph K., for without having done anything wrong he was arrested one morning.

8 To the red country and part of the gray country of Oklahoma the last rains came gently, and they did not cut the scarred earth.

9 It was a bright cold day in April and the clocks were striking thirteen.

10 Nobody could sleep. When morning came, assault craft would be lowered and a first wave of troops would ride through the surf and charge ashore on the beach at Anopopei.

11 The past is a foreign country: they do things differently there.

12 I can see by my watch without taking my hand from the left grip

of the cycle, that it is eight-thirty in the morning.

13 It was five o'clock on a winter's morning in Syria. Alongside the platform at Aleppo stood the train grandly designated in railway guides as the Taurus Express.

14 I first met Dean not long after my wife and I split up.

15 It is cold at six-forty in the morning of a March day in Paris, and seems even colder when a man is about to be executed by firing squad.

16 As the streets that lead from the Strand to the Embankment are very narrow, it is better not to walk down them arm-in-arm.

17 In the spring of 1917, when Doctor Richard Diver first arrived in Zurich, he was twenty-six years old, a fine age for a man, indeed the very acme of bachelorhood.

18 I wish either my father or my mother, or indeed both of them, as they were in duty equally bound to it, had minded what they were about when they begot me.

19 We were in the preparation room when the head came in, followed by a new boy in ordinary clothes, and by a school servant carrying a large desk.

20 All happy families resemble one another, but each unhappy family is unhappy in its own way.

(See Answers on page 261.)

# I

## BEFORE E?

When, years ago and very briefly, I taught English at the Park School in Baltimore, Maryland, I encouraged my students to learn what I had always regarded as one of the basic rules of spelling: "It's *I* before *E* except after *C*."

And so it is with *piece* and *receipt* and a multitude of other words. But unfortunately for me – and all the other English teachers who want a quiet life – it seems this time-honoured rule isn't as reliable as we thought. The English language turns out to be riddled with words in which an *E* comes before an *I* and there's no *C* to be seen and in which an *I* comes before an *E* immediately after a *C*.

If you need proof that rules are made to be broken, here it is:

ageism
agencies
ancient
beige
being
Beirut
caffeine
codeine
conscience
counterfeit
deficient
deign
Deirdre
efficient
eider
eighth
either
Fahrenheit
fancied
feign
feint
financier
foreign
forfeit
freight
geisha
glacier

heifer
heinous
heir
Hygeia
inveigle
Keith
Leicester
leishmaniasis
leisure
Marcie
mercies
monteith
neigh
neighbour
Neil
neither
nonpareil
nuclei
obeisance
omniscient
onomatopoeic
pharmacopoeia
plebeian
Pleiades
policies
poltergeist
proficient

reimburse
rein
reindeer
reitbok
science
seize
sheik
Sheila
skein
sleigh
sovereign
species
sufficient
surfeit
tenancies
their
theism
unpolicied
veiled
vein
weigh
weir
weird
Weissnichtwo
zein

To make matters twice as bad, here are a dozen words where the golden rule is broken not once but twice:

alliciencies
anciencies
cleidomancies
deficiencies

efficiencies
Einstein
omnisciencies
oneiromancies

pleistoseist                    sufficiencies
proficiencies                   Zeitgeist

Okay, so *Einstein's* a name and *Zeitgeist* isn't English, but you get the point – or is it *piont*? Spelling never was my strong suit.

## A FINE SPELL

To find out how good you are at the spelling game, take a look at this list of forty-nine words. Alternative spellings are given for each word. What you have to do is work out which of the two versions is the correct one. A score of 20 is adequate for a school leaver, 30 is acceptable for a graduate, 40 is excellent, and 49 unbelievable – or is it *unbeleivable*?

| | | | |
|---|---|---|---|
| accomodation | accommodation | | |
| battallion | battalion | naphtha | naptha |
| broccoli | brocolli | occurrence | occurence |
| cemetary | cemetery | parafin | paraffin |
| Chihuahua | Chihuhua | parallel | paralell |
| coliseum | colisseum | plausible | plausable |
| connoisseur | connoiseur | pseudonymous | pseudonymious |
| coxwain | coxswain | quintessence | quintessance |
| desiccate | dessicate | rarefy | rarify |
| ecstasy | ecstacy | reconnaissance | reconaissance |
| elemosynary | eleemosynary | renaissance | rennaissance |
| embarass | embarrass | sacreligious | sacrilegious |
| fettucine | fettuccine | sangfroid | sangfroiod |
| gneis | gneiss | shillelagh | shilailie |
| guilotine | guillotine | subpoenaed | subpoened |
| haemorhage | haemorrhage | supersede | superseed |
| hypocricy | hypocrisy | threshhold | threshold |
| idiosyncrasy | idiosyncracy | ukelele | ukelelle |
| jubilee | jubillee | vermillion | vermilion |
| kwashiorkor | kwashiokor | vichysoise | vichyssoise |
| myrrh | myrhh | victual | vitual |

| | | | |
|---|---|---|---|
| liaison | liasion | weltschmerz | welschmertz |
| liquefy | liquify | Xanthippe | Xanthipe |
| mischievous | mischeivous | yashmack | yashmak |
| moccasin | mocassin | zabagllione | zabaglione |

(See Answers, page 261.)

## ORIGINAL SPELLING

Some words look as if they have been misspelled when they haven't been. Here is a selection – or is it *sellection*?

*Astroid* is not a misspelling of *asteroid* but an adjective meaning "star-shaped".

*Contect* is not a misspelling of *context* but a verb meaning "to cover".

*Crysal* is not a misspelling of *crystal* but a part of an archery bow.

*Galop* is not a misspelling of *gallop* but a nineteenth-century German dance.

*Harras* is not a misspelling of *harass* but a herd of stud horses.

*Housebote* is not a misspelling of *houseboat* but wood allowed to a tenant for repairing a house.

*Merengue* is not a misspelling of *meringue* but a popular Dominican and Haitian ballroom dance.

*Orchestia* is not a misspelling of *orchestra* but a genus of crustaceans, including beach fleas.

*Orignal* is not a misspelling of *original* but is the American moose.

*Rictal* is not a misspelling of *rectal* but an adjective meaning "relating to the mouth orifice".

*Roadeo* is not a misspelling of *rodeo* but a contest featuring events that test driving skill.

*Starlite* is not a misspelling of *starlight* but a blue zircon, a type of mineral.

*Tecnology* is not a misspelling of *technology* but the study of children.

*Tradevman* is not a misspelling of *tradesman* but a petty officer in the US Navy.

*Viraginity* is not a misspelling of *virginity* but the character of a virago – a bold, shrewish woman.

*Warehous* is not a misspelling of *warehouse* but the plural of *warehou*, a fish from Australia and New Zealand.

*Warfarin* is not a misspelling of *warfaring* but a chemical compound used as a rodenticide.

*Windrow* is not a misspelling of *window* but a row of hay, raked together to dry.

*Zilwaukee* is not a misspelling of *Milwaukee* but a town in Saginaw County, Michigan.

# HYPHENATION HYPE

Words – like *half-life* – that use one hyphen are common enough. Words that need two hyphens – like mother-in-law – aren't unusual either. But finding words that require three hyphens or more isn't easy.

Here are nine, most of them names of plants or flowers:

### 3 HYPHENS

*Snow-on-the-mountain* is a spurge of the western United States that has showy flower clusters and is used ornamentally.

### 4 HYPHENS

*Gill-go-by-the-ground* is a trailing Eurasian mint that is common as a weed in North America.

**5 HYPHENS**

*John-go-to-bed-at-noon* is any of several plants whose flowers close about noon.

*Kiss-me-over-the-garden-gate* is any of various plants, especially prince's-feather.

**7 HYPHENS**

*Har-u-pu-ka-ka-sharu-sha-bau* is the name of a mystical Egyptian deity.

**8 HYPHENS**

*Willy-with-the-wisp-and-Peggy-with-the-lantern* is a light that appears at night over marshy ground.

**9 HYPHENS**

*Great-great-great-great-great-great-grand-niece-in-law* is a relation; this particular term appears in the *Oxford English Dictionary* as an illustrative quotation given under *great* from John Lockhart's book *Reginald Dalton*: "that old body that says she is Shakespeare's great-great-great-great-great-great-grand-niece-in-law".

*Kitty-come-down-the-lane-jump-up-and-kiss-me* is the cuckoo-pint, a common European arum.

*Meet-her-in-the-entry-kiss-her-in-the-buttery* is another flower: a pansy.

The three words that have nine hyphens are the only three of their kind I've been able to find, and I have not come across a single word that has ten hyphens. If you happen to discover a not-four-five-six-seven-eight-or-nine-but-ten-legged word listed in any legitimate dictionary, do let me know.

# G OOD AS A GOLDFISH

Samuel Goldfish (1882–1974) had a winning way with words. Polish by birth, he became an American citizen, changed his name to Samuel Goldwyn, and grew to be one of the legendary Hollywood movie moguls. Almost as memorable as the great MGM pictures he produced were the great verbal clangers he created.

An agent once tried to sell Goldwyn a prominent actor. Goldwyn replied that he was not interested in established stars: he wanted to build his own stars instead.

"Look how I developed Jon Hall," said Goldwyn. "He's a better leading man than Robert Taylor will ever be – some day."

Goldwynisms are unique because they are turns of phrase that manage to make some sense and no sense at all at one and the same time. In my Goldwyn Book of Quotes these are the gems that would have pride of place.

"Every director bites the hand that lays the golden egg."

"A verbal contract isn't worth the paper it's written on."

"You ought to take the bull between the teeth."

"We're overpaying him but he's worth it."

"Why should people go out and pay good money to see bad films when they can stay at home and see bad television for nothing?"

"We have all passed a lot of water since then."

"How'm I gonna do decent pictures when all my good writers are in jail? Don't misunderstand me, they all ought to be hung."

"Chaplin is no businessman – all he knows is he can't take anything less."

"We want a story that starts with an earthquake and works its way up to a climax."

"My Toujours Lautrec!"

"Tell me, how did you love my picture?"

"Yes, my wife's hands are very beautiful. I'm going to have a bust made of them."

"Anybody who goes to see a psychiatrist ought to have his head examined."

When working on a motion picture of the life of Christ: "Why only twelve disciples? Go and get thousands."

"Gentlemen, I want you to know that I am not always right, but I am never wrong."

"If Roosevelt were alive he'd turn over in his grave."

"I'll give you a definite maybe."

"The reason why so many people turned up at Louis B. Mayer's funeral was they wanted to make sure he was dead."

"It's more than magnificent – it's mediocre."

"If you cannot give me your word of honour will you give me your promise?"

When told that a story was rather caustic he replied: "I don't care what it costs. If it's good, we'll make it."

Of a book: "I read part of it all the way through."

Of a piece of dialogue: "Let's have some new clichés."

"A bachelor's life is no life for a single man."

"A wide screen just makes a bad film twice as bad."

"Going to call him 'William'? What kind of a name is that? Every Tom, Dick and Harry's called William. Why don't you call him Bill?"

"In two words: im-possible."

# F<br>RENCH WITHOUT TEARS

> Imagine the Lord talking French! Aside from a few odd words in Hebrew, I took it completely for granted that God had never spoken anything but the most dignified English.

Clarence Day was right. God speaks English – always has done, always will. And it's probably because they want to keep on the right side of the Almighty that the French have started to bring English words into their vocabulary.

The language of *haute cuisine* was once exclusively French, but nowadays at almost any Paris restaurant you can order *le fast food, le banana split, le biftek*, and *le chips* – which is what we British call french fries.

In the world of sport Frenchmen now speak of *le fair-play, le soccer*, and *les jockeys*. Sometimes their thinking gets a little muddled – *un jerk* is a good dancer, *un scratcher* is a great

golfer, and *un egghead* is an imbecile – but on the whole they
are on *le right track*.

Even their poetry is beginning to sound English. Read these
three gems out loud and you will see – and hear – what I mean.

> Un petit d'un petit
> S'étonne aux Halles
> Un petit d'un petit
> Ah! degrés te fallent
> Indolent qui ne sort cesse
> Indolent qui ne se mène
> Qu'importe un petit d'un petit
> Tout Gai de Reguennes.

> Reine, reine, guex éveille.
> Gomme à gaine, en horreur, taie.

> Oh, Anne, doux
> But, Cueilles ma chou.
> Trille fort,
> Chatte dort.
> Faveux Sikhs,
> Pie coupe Styx.
> Sève nette,
> Les dèmes se traitent.
> N'a ne d'haine,
> Ecoute, fée daine.

> Eléphant tue elfes
> Dit qu'en Delft.
> Tartines, fortunes,
> Miséricorde d'une.
> Fit vetimes Sixtine
> Médicine quitte Chine.
> C'est Fantine est d'Inn
> Mais Arouet dine.
> Nanini, Toine est dit,
> Met platres, sème petit.

# E
## PISTLES AT DAWN

I once met a man who had won a fortune on the Pools. I asked him what he did about all the begging letters. "Oh, I keep on sending them," he said.

I'm not fond of begging letters, but I don't mind hate mail. If you enjoy reading other people's acid epistles you'll like these.

### TO TV-AM, LONDON

Dear Sirs, I have watched your programme daily for almost a year and I can hardly believe that the planet earth can contain so many self-satisfied, suppurating snotbags as you have managed to gather in one place at one time. They are without exception verminous, vile and quite appallingly *voluble*. The worst by far is Giles Brandworth [*sic*] a priggish, pop-eyed, pompous popinjay who should have been drowned at birth by his mother's husband – had she had one, which I doubt. Thanking you for your kind attention. . . .

TO THE CBS TV NETWORK, NEW YORK

What in hell is the matter with your news team?

What was so damned amusing about the item concerning the lost mother cat with the amputated tail? To the concerned owners there was nothing very hilarious about it.

The whole news team repeatedly smirks and grins even after a report of a tragic incident in the news.

Don't tell me they have a irrepressible sense of humor. So do little boys and girls in the third grade.

TO THE EDITOR OF THE *KENYA STANDARD*

Sir, if you print any more photographs of naked women, I shall cease borrowing your newspaper.

And it's not just we mere media hacks who are on the receiving end of caustic correspondence. The sainted Abraham Lincoln received this letter at the White House:

God damn your god damned old hellfired god damned soul to hell god damn you and god damn your god damned family's god damned hellfired god damned soul to hell and god damnation god damn them and god damn your god damned friends to hell.

## TOP MARX

Groucho Marx was one of the century's most prolific and entertaining letter writers. As a correspondent he was more quirky than caustic, as these three, typical, letters show.

TO SAM ZOLOTOW OF *THE NEW YORK TIMES* DRAMA DEPARTMENT

December 5, 1945

Dear Sam,

My plans are still in embryo. In case you've never been there, this is a small town on the outskirts of wishful thinking. At the moment, I'm deep in the heart of *Casablanca* and it's thrilling work. I arise at seven every morning, kick the alarm clock in the groin and speed to the studio. I always get a nine o'clock call, which means I shoot promptly at three in the afternoon. There's no use protesting –

this is the way the movie business is geared and I suspect that's the chief reason why so much bilge appears in your neighborhood theater.

Yours,
Groucho

TO HOWARD HUGHES

January 23, 1951

Dear Mr. Hughes,

Between retooling for the war effort and dueling with Wald and Krasna, I presume you are a fairly busy man. However, I wonder if you could spare a few moments to release a picture that was made some years ago involving Jane Russell, Frank Sinatra and your correspondent. The name of the picture, if memory serves, is *It's Only Money*. I never did see it but I have been told that at its various previews it was received with considerable enthusiasm.

I am not a young man any more, Mr. Hughes, and before I shuffle off this mortal coil if you could see your way clear to pry open the strong box and send this minor masterpiece whizzing through the film exchanges of America, you would not only have earned my undying gratitude but that of the United Nations, the popcorn dealers of America and the three RKO stockholders who at the moment are trying to escape from the Mellon Bank of Pittsburgh.

Sincerely,
Groucho Marx

TO T.S. ELIOT

June 19, 1961

Dear T. S.,

Your photograph arrived in good shape and I hope this note of thanks finds you in the same condition.

I had no idea you were so handsome. Why you haven't been offered the lead in some sexy movies I can only attribute to the stupidity of the casting directors.

Should I come to London I will certainly take advantage of your kind invitation and if you come to California I hope you will allow me to do the same.

Cordially,
Groucho Marx

## LETTERS PLAY

Some of the most intriguing and important letters ever written weren't – if you see what I mean. Take a look at these historic documents, recently discovered by the historian and wit Michael Green.

*From*: Napoléon Bonaparte, Emperor of the French; First Consul for Life; First Citizen of France; King *in absentia* of the United Kingdom of Great Britain and Ireland; Commander-in-Chief of the Imperial Grand Army of France; Commander of the First Military District; Commander of the Second Military District; Commander of the Third Military District; Colonel-in-Chief of the Old Guard; Head of the Deuxième Bureau; Controller of the Troisième Bureau; Commander of the Légion d'Honneur; Chief of the Imperial Order of St. Anthony; holder of the Médaille Militaire with oak leaves; holder of the award for meritorious service (with branches).

*To*: The Empress Joséphine of all France; Queen *in absentia* of the United Kingdom of Great Britain and Ireland; Grande Dame of the Imperial Order of St. Anthony.

Tilsit, Saturday

Tonight, Joséphine.

Boney

*From*: The Empress Joséphine of all France; Queen *in absentia* of the United Kingdom and Ireland; Grande Dame of the Imperial Order of St. Anthony.

*To*: Napoléon Bonaparte, Emperor of the French; First Consul for Life; First Citizen of France; King *in absentia* of the United Kingdom of Great Britain and Ireland; Commander-in-Chief of the Imperial Grand Army of France; Commander of the First Military District; Commander of the Second Military District; Commander of the Third Military District; Colonel-in-Chief of the Old Guard; Head of the Deuxième Bureau; Controller of the Troisième Bureau; Commander of the Légion d'Honneur; Chief of the Imperial Order of St. Anthony; holder of the Médaille Militaire with oak leaves; holder of the award for meritorious service (with branches).

Sorry, headache.

Joséphine

# D

## UNROAMIN

Whatever you call it – Dunroamin or Buckingham Palace, The White House or Mon Repos – if you give your house a name you give it an extra dimension. Whether you live in a tiny apartment with just one room or the world's largest house (Biltmore House in Asheville, North Carolina, with 250 rooms), when you give your home a name you help give it an identity.

Some people are more ingenious than others at finding apt names for their home. There's a distinguished family of musicians called the Skeapings who called their home "Finders" and an equally inventive couple called Adam and Eve Orchard (this is true) who named their house "Eden End".

To help you name or rename your home, here are twenty suggestions. They are all names that belong to real houses, and I have supplied explanatory notes as appropriate.

| | |
|---|---|
| *Alcrest* | After *l*abour comes *rest*. |
| *Bachelor's Adventure* | A holiday home. |
| *Billion* | Owned by Bill and Marion. |
| *Bonanza* | Spanish for *prosperity*. |
| *Copper Coin* | What was left in the bank after the purchase. |
| *Dalsida* | Home of a *Dal*matian, a *Si*amese, and a Great *Da*ne. |
| *Elveston* | Anagram of *lovenest*. |
| *Erzanmine* | Ours. |
| *Fortitoo* | 42. |
| *Hangover Hall* | Seen in Temperance road. |
| *Lucky Dip* | Holiday house at the beach. |
| *Mews Cottage* | Home of pampered cat. |
| *Morning Feeling* | Occupied by the Munday family. |
| *Spooks* | Opposite the cemetery. |
| *The Chimes* | Home of the Bell family. |
| *The Pride* | Where the Lyons family lives. |
| *The Struggle* | Until the mortgage is cleared. |
| *Tivuli* | A back-spelling. |
| *Traynes* | Near the railway line. |
| *Number Ten* | A good address. |

# C RAZY CROSSWORDS

It's CROSS CRAZY WORDS. No it isn't. It's WORDY CROSS-CRAZES. No it isn't. It's COZY WORDSCARES. No it isn't. It's WORSE CRAZYCODES. No it isn't. It's *CRAZY CROSSWORDS*. Yes it is!

### THE WORLD'S SMALLEST CROSSWORD

The world's largest crossword was devised by a Belgian called Henri Blaise. It contained 25,000 squares, featured 7,748 clues, and took Monsieur Blaise eight years to compile. I wanted to share it with you, but I didn't have the room. The crossword grid alone measures nearly nineteen square feet.

Instead I am offering you an original puzzle of my own. It's the world's smallest crossword and comes complete with a couple of suitably cryptic clues.

ACROSS
1 Time of deranged pride encompassing nothing.

DOWN
1 A marriage portion from a small Dutch coin that I leave.

(See Answers on page 262.)

## AN AUSTRALIAN CROSSWORD

Here's another unusual crossword, with cryptic clues to match.

ACROSS
1 Time spent Down Under.

DOWN
1 Soundly a measure of print.
2 Hear that one is in debt.
3 Hero found after being deserted by her.
4 Australian end.

(See Answers on page 262.)

## AN IRISH CROSSWORD

4 Knock one anyway you like, and one will get it off one correctly.

(See Answers on page 260.)

# A FLUID CROSSWORD

ACROSS
1 A hunchbacked puppet with a hooked nose.
6 A short-legged round-bodied horse bred in England.
7 To drive cattle in the USA.
8 To thump or strike.
9 A type of tool.

DOWN
1 Sound vegetables.
2 Sound sheep.
3 Sound measures of print.
4 Sound of Black, Red, White and Yellow marine regions.
5 Hydrogen in brief, times five.

And why is it a *fluid* crossword?

(See Answers on page 265.)

## A SIBILANT CROSSWORD

William Sunners loves the nineteenth letter of the alphabet, and here's a crossword of his to prove it.

ACROSS
1 Shrieks.
5 Stories.
10 Section.
14 Seclude.
15 Site.
16 Stint.
17 Select.
18 Sinister side.
19 Subdues.
20 Solution.
22 Schooled sufficiently.
24 Swallows sustenance.
26 Specific sum sought.
27 Solanaceous shrub.
31 Stormy sea swell.
35 Strong spite.
36 Screened sharpshooting.
38 Strained situation.
39 Shears.
41 Steeple.
43 Starch.
44 Salt.
46 Scarcely sufficient.
48 Situated.
49 Savage sovereign.
51 Startlers.
53 Strong shipbuilding staves.
55 Singer.
56 Settle; set; steady.
60 Speech.
64 Sewing stitch.
65 Sorrow.
67 Street, surface.
68 Seed shell.
69 Spear.
70 Sign.
71 Sound.
72 Stopper.
73 Sunken spot.

DOWN
1 Stupor.
2 Sanction.
3 Scholars.
4 Seethed.
5 Stoic sufferers.
6 Summit.
7 Sinners' structure.
8 Sharp; stinging.
9 Saw set.
10 Scares.
11 State.
12 Stinted sustenance.
13 Suggested substitute.
21 Sound sensitizers.
23 Sable.
25 Springs.
27 Studied simulation.
28 Stopped sitting.
29 Salamanders.
30 Stately scanned songs.
32 Sub-let.
33 Shakespearean sorrowful
   sovereign's son.
34 Soil strivers.
37 Semi-sacred song safeguarded.
40 Sevenfold.
42 Smooth surfaces prayer.
45 Spawns.
47 Snare.
50 Speak slanderously.
52 Stand.
54 Sacred.
56 Sorrowful statement.
57 Springbok-like species.
58 Stamp.
59 Sense.
61 Steel sheet.
62 Stove.
63 Servant's superior (slang).
66 Skilful skywayman.

(See Answers on page 263.)

## AN ANAGRAMMATIC CROSSWORD

I asked my friend Dave Crossland to create a couple of tough puzzles for this chapter, and he hasn't let me down. In this one all the clues are cryptic, and the across solutions have to be made into anagrams before they are inserted in the diagram. For example, if the intermediate solution to an across clue was TACIT, the letters could be rearranged to form the actual answer, ATTIC. You will be relieved to know that the down solutions are normal.

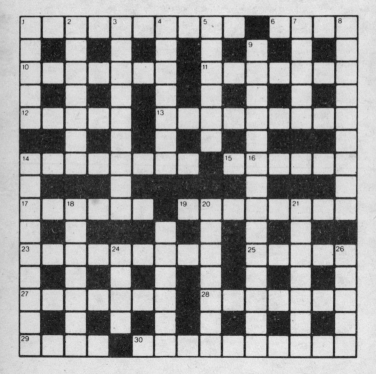

ACROSS

1 Very orderly worker is tense during heavy work? (10)
6 Fail to stand upright, being very thin. (4)
10 Rather rude convict, outwardly nonreligious. (7)
11 Save receipt, lady? That's mean. (7)
12 Sweeper having skirmish. (5)
13 Words put together to form courtly judgments. (9)
14 Full-time team in split. (8)
15 Bill joins two returning soaks. (6)
17 Lurking in steep lane there's a ceaseless traveller. (6)
19 Urgently wanting new design to include Rhode Island. (8)
23 Roman office gives praise about North America. (9)
25 Chemical temperature must be kept in check? Quite the reverse. (5)
27 Cyrus gets around the French displaying degree of attractiveness. (7)
28 Behold one, not completely elegant, dawdles. (7)
29 Observe a piece of music. (4)
30 To sing about milliner is causing great upset. (10)

DOWN

1 Exhibition of skills given by experts on piano. (5)
2 Neglects abandoned regions. (7)
3 Disease caused by parasites that orbit neck cunningly? (4–5)
4 Female turning up greets electorate, though not the whole lot. (7)
5 Appointing North American dynasty of old. (6)
7 Bowmen decapitated demonstrators. (7)
8 Conductor, one specially chosen, took a ride. (9)
9 Man of rank – king – raised dagger. (4)
14 I'm one in need of treatment, showing intolerance. (9)
16 Recovering, say, during exercise (having lost head). (9)
18 Foreigner, French one, thrown into a jail. (7)
20 Inactivity? Wrong, I train with small amount of energy. (7)
21 Plead, in old-fashioned way, during free entertainment. (7)
22 Most recent fashion stimulates trend within. (6)
24 I governed a country. (4)
26 Enchanted siren in more elevated place? (5)

(See Answers on page 263.)

## A CROSSWORD WITH MISPRINTS

There is a misprint of one letter in the definition part of each across clue (e.g. if the definition word was printed as DENTAL, the correct definition might be DENIAL). Answers are to be inserted correctly. Down clues are normal, but solutions are to be entered with one letter misprinted: the misprinted letter occurs always where the down word intersects with an across one, and the misprinted form of the solution is always a word in its own right.

ACROSS

1 Chap, Canadian, is thinner. (7)

5 Established in fort, actors took charge. (7)

9 Result of mending cord – first pull one on. (9)

10 Hastily elect leaders of the Unionist Party after race. (3, 2)

11 Receives black sections of sail. (6)

12 I caper and pass wanderer hiding identity. (8)

14 Smells in apartments around the East. (8)

15 Shell guided first pair of geologists. (5)

18 Chimp gives fwee entertainment, it's said. (5)

20 Snows at hand on the Sabbath. (8)

23 First person, we hear, dances in stages. (8)

25 Very cold coves, one centigrade – take a step back. (3–3)

27 Food means nothing in early part of day. (5)

28 Trap siren with cunning, and swear. (9)

29 Gentleman trapped in action is wasted. (7)

30 Striker observed lots of people on backstreet of Paris. (7)

DOWN

1 Regions of one hundred fruit trees. (6)

2 Wealth enables a barrier to be put around virus. (9)

3 Attentive male sorted out feud over lady. (7)

4 South African currency obtained in Iran, dubiously. (4)

5 Came to an agreement (abridged?). (10)

6 Freed from sin, shiver, trembling, before last part of absolution. (7)

7 Satan, rising up, was far from dead. (5)

8 Gave account that went off with a bang? (8)

13 Made report about one tailless hybrid being aroused. (10)

16 I have gone on to desert the cause, showing signs of imperfection. (9)

17 Rushed, upset. (8)

19 Short film of mobile home. (7)

21 Imprisons first of ghosts during awful seance. (7)

22 University supporting army regulation creates commotion. (6)

24 Cautions, normal in battles. (5)

26 Steady business enterprise. (4)

(See Answers on page 264.)

# B URGER POWER

Gazing at the typewriter in moments of desperation ("Mrs Beeton died at twenty-eight. I'm thirty-nine and what have I done?"), hitting the typewriter in moments of black despair ("Keats died at twenty-five; I'm pushing forty, and what have I done?"), I console myself with three thoughts: a drink at six, dinner at eight, and to be immortal you've got to be dead.

I'm alive and I adore food and drink. To me they're very real pleasures indeed (and I'm delighted to hear from my elders that they're also the pleasures that last), and because I find them such fun I'm able to use food as a carrot and drink as a carrot juice (?) in the never-ending struggle to get my work done. As writers go, I'm quite disciplined: I set myself a target of so many words an hour, and if I get behind schedule I don't give myself a break until I've caught up. On "writing days" I have a light lunch and never drink until the day's work is done. With my first book, I had a celebratory meal at the end of every chapter. Now I've written so many, I don't celebrate until the whole book is done.

In the matter of food, as with everything else, I'm a very lucky individual. I live with one of the world's great cooks. I eat like a king – quite literally, at times, since my wife has made a speciality of the favourite dishes of English monarchs since the Norman Conquest. Here's a recipe for a princely dessert that I love. I admit that "Quyncys in Compost" isn't the most appetizing of titles, but once tried it's never forgotten. And it's a dish that's stood the test of time: Henry VI (aged eight) had it at his Coronation banquet in 1422.

You will need: 2 ½ ounces whole stem ginger; 3 fluid ounces sherry; 22 fluid ounces red wine; 4 quinces or large, firm pears; 8 ounces caster sugar; 8 ounces stoned dates; 2 level teaspoons ground cinnamon; 1 level teaspoon ground ginger; a pinch of salt.

Cut the ginger into thin slices and leave to soak in the sherry in a covered jar for three days.

Peel the quinces or pears and slice into rounds about one-quarter inch thick. Remove core from each piece of fruit. Dissolve the sugar gently in the wine and heat until the syrup starts to thicken (about 15 minutes). Add the fruit to the wine and simmer gently until cooked but still firm (about 10 minutes). Add the dates, spices, and salt. Continue heating without boiling until the flavours are thoroughly blended. Taste, and add more sugar if necessary. The wine should have a syrupy consistency and the fruit should be firm. Leave to cool.

Strain the ginger, reserving a tablespoon of the liquid. Stir this and the ginger into the wine syrup. Serve well chilled. (*Serves 6.*)

When I'm not eating like an English king, I'm eating like a modern American. Man cannot live by bread alone, which is why he puts meat next to it and calls it a hamburger. There must be Macdonald blood in my veins, because show me a burger and my mouth starts to water. What's more, not only do I eat burgers of every kind with relish (and without), I also collect their names.

Here are forty that I've come across. Lick your lips and read on:

baconburger
barbecueburger
beefburger
catfish-burger *
cheeseburger
chicken-burger
chilli-burger
Chinese-burger (containing rice)
chuckburger
clamburger
dogburger
double-burger (two hamburgers in one bun)
eggburger
fishburger
glutenburger *
griddleburger (browned on a griddle)
horsemeatburger *
huskiburger *
jamburgo (a Mexican spelling of *hamburger* – not a hamburger served with jam)
kirschburger *
lamburger (made of ground lamb)
liver-sausage-burger
liverwurst-burger
nutburger
oomphburger (a hamburger served with oomph!)
pickleburger
porkburger
rabbitburger *
seaburger *
Spamburger (made from a proprietary tinned meat, Spam)
tomatoburger

*These I've heard about but haven't eaten. All the rest I unreservedly recommend.

# A IEE!

I like unusual words, and the more unusual they are the more I like them. That's why I've leafed through *Webster's Third New International Dictionary* to find the hundred most unusual and – to me – most likable words in the English language.

Here they are:

| | |
|---|---|
| *aiee* | An interjection of grief. |
| *axolotl* | A salamander. |
| *bdelloid* | Like a leech. |
| *cnemial* | Relating to the shin. |
| *crwth* | An ancient Celtic musical instrument. |
| *csardas* | A Hungarian dance. |
| *ctetology* | A branch of biology. |

| | |
|---|---|
| *cwm* | A basin on a mountainside. |
| *dghaisa* | A small boat of Malta. |
| *dhikr* | A ritual formula. |
| *dirndl* | A style of dress. |
| *djebel* | A hill in northern Africa. |
| *dukhn* | A cereal grass of Africa and Asia. |
| *dukw* | An amphibious vehicle. |
| *dvandva* | A compound word. |
| *dwam* | To become dazed. |
| *dzeren* | A gazelle of Asia. |
| *eebree* | An eyebrow. |
| *Firbolg* | An early people of Ireland. |
| *forjaskit* | Exhausted. |
| *fremd* | Unrelated. |
| *gjetost* | A hard dark-brown cheese made from goat's milk. |
| *gmelinite* | A mineral. |
| *gwyniad* | A Welsh fish. |
| *gyttja* | A type of mud containing organic material. |
| *hamsocn* | Burglary or housebreaking. |
| *hheth* | The eighth letter of the Hebrew alphabet. |
| *hjelmite* | A mineral. |
| *hsin* | In Confucianism, the cardinal virtue of faithfulness. |
| *humuhumunukunu-kuapuaa* | A small Hawaiian fish. |
| *hwan* | The basic monetary unit of South Korea. |
| *iao* | An Australian bird. |
| *ieie* | A pine of the Pacific Islands. |
| *ioa* | A sea bird chiefly found in tropical seas. |
| *ixodid* | A tick. |
| *iynx* | A woodpecker. |
| *jheel* | A pool, marsh, or lake of India. |
| *jnana* | Knowledge. |

| | |
|---|---|
| *kjeldahlization* | A particular chemical process. |
| *Kpelle* | A people of central Liberia. |
| *Kshatriya* | A twice-born Hindu. |
| *kthibh* | A type of reading in the Hebrew Bible. |
| *kvass* | A beer. |
| *Kwalhioqua* | A people of southwestern Washington State. |
| *kokerboom* | The quiver tree. |
| *kwatuma* | Any of several eels of southern Africa. |
| *kyoodle* | To holler, to yap. |
| *lamedh* | The twelfth letter of the Hebrew alphabet. |
| *Lwena* | A Bantu language. |
| *mbori* | A camel disease. |
| *mlechchha* | One who does not practise Hinduism. |
| *Mpongwe* | Another Bantu language. |
| *msasa* | Any of various African trees. |
| *mwami* | The ruler or king of Ruanda-Urundi (now Rwanda and Burundi) in East Africa. |
| *Mzabite* | A Berber people of the Algerian Sahara. |
| *naumkeag* | A machine for smoothing the soles and heels of shoes. |
| *ngege* | An important African food fish. |
| *njave* | A very large tropical African tree. |
| *Nkole* | Another Bantu language. |
| *nritya* | A type of dance of India. |
| *nsambya* | An African timber tree. |
| *ollamh* | A learned man in ancient Ireland. |
| *o-o-a-a* | A bird from the Hawaiian island of Kauai. |
| *ouabaio* | A tree of southern Africa. |
| *piobaireachd* | Elaborate tunes for the Scottish Highland bagpipes. |
| *pneumonoultramicro-scopicsilicovolcano-coniosis* | A miner's lung disease. |
| *qutb* | An Islamic saint. |
| *ramfeezled* | Exhausted. |

| | |
|---|---|
| *rsi* | A holy Hindu sage. |
| *rta* | A specific principle. |
| *sdrucciola* | A musical term. |
| *sferics* | Atmospherics. |
| *sjogrenite* | A mineral. |
| *smaragd* | Emerald. |
| *squdge* | Ooze. |
| *sravaka* | A direct disciple of Buddha. |
| *szikite* | A mineral. |
| *tehaviche* | The king salmon. |
| *tfillin* | The phylacteries worn by Jews. |
| *tjaele* | Frozen ground. |
| *tlac* | A small copper coin of nineteenth-century Mexico. |
| *tmesis* | Separation of the parts of a compound word. |
| *tnoyim* | A Jewish social function. |
| *tomnoddy* | A fool. |
| *tryptyque* | A customs pass. |
| *tsantsa* | A shrunken head. |
| *tzut* | A brightly patterned square of cotton worn as a head covering. |
| *uang* | A rhinoceros beetle. |
| *ucuuba* | A Brazilian tree. |
| *uwarowite* | An emerald-green garnet. |
| *vly* | A temporary lake. |
| *voeu* | A proposal. |
| *vrille* | An aeroplane manoeuvre |
| *yclept* | Named. |
| *ynambu* | A very large bird of southern Brazil. |
| *yperite* | Mustard gas. |
| *yttrium* | A chemical element. |
| *zikr* | The same as *dhikr*. |
| *zloty* | The basic monetary unit of Poland. |
| *zwieback* | A sweetened bread. |

## UNIQUE DARRYL

I like dictionaries, but my friend Darryl Francis is demented about them. Recently he waded through fifteen of the world's leading English dictionaries simply to find a word in each that wasn't in any of the others.

Locating one word that is unique to each of the fifteen dictionaries was no easy task. Selecting a likely word from a particular dictionary and then checking it against the other fourteen usually revealed that the word *did* appear in at least one of the others – often the twelfth, thirteenth, or fourteenth. In his search Darryl made countless false starts. For example, he thought *gallerygoer* was unique to *Webster's New Collegiate* (8th edition) until he found the hyphenated form, *gallery-goer*, in the *Oxford English Dictionary*, though not as a main entry. He thought *Eastralia* was unique to the 1909 edition of *Webster's* until he found it tucked away in the supplement to the *Century Dictionary*. *Kgotla*, in the H-N Supplement of the *Oxford English Dictionary*, looked as if it might be unique, but it then turned up in *Chambers*. He expected *complexification* in the 1934 *Webster's* to be unique as it hadn't been included in the 1961 *Webster's*, but no! The A-G Supplement of the *Oxford English Dictionary* also lists *complexification*.

Darryl is one of those verbivores who doesn't give in easily and eventually he made it. Thanks to his persistence, *The Joy of Lex* can now proudly present the fifteen unique words that are featured once and once only in fifteen of the world's most important dictionaries.

Here they are:

*The Century Dictionary* (1897)

bamlite      A variety of fibrolite, a subsilicate of aluminium, from Bamle, Norway.

*The Century Dictionary Supplement* (1909)

pisang-ayer     The traveller's-tree of the East Indies.

*Chambers Twentieth Century Dictionary* (1977)

gju      A kind of violin used in the Shetland Isles of Scotland.

*Concise Oxford Dictionary* (6th edition, 1976)

*antivivisectionism*     Opposition to vivisection.

*Funk & Wagnall's New Standard Dictionary* (1946)

*zij*     The Persian astronomical tables, revised and corrected by Omar Khayyam.

*The Oxford English Dictionary* (1933)

*steeplet*     A small steeple.

Supplement to *The Oxford English Dictionary* (1933)

*witchologist*     One who studies witches or witchcraft.

A-G Supplement to *The Oxford English Dictionary* (1972)

*deproletarianizable*     Able to be freed of proletarian character or qualities.

H-N Supplement to *The Oxford English Dictionary* (1976)

*jazzophile*     A devotee of jazz.

*Random House Dictionary* (1966)

*fiqh*     In Islam, jurisprudence based on theology.

*Webster's New International Dictionary* (1st edition, 1909)

*fabrikona*     A variety of canvas wall hanging.

*Webster's New International Dictionary* (2nd edition, 1934)

*Taeniodontidae*     A family of Lower Eocene edentates, certain toothless prehistoric mammals.

*Webster's Third New International Dictionary* (1961)

*rta*     The cosmic-moral principle of order that in Vedic tradition establishes regularity and righteousness in the world.

*Webster's New Collegiate Dictionary* (8th edition, 1973)

*buqsha*     A monetary unit of the Yemen, 40 buqshas to the rial.

*Collins English Dictionary* (1979)

*twp*    A Welsh dialect word meaning "stupid".

## MISH MASH

Darryl Francis has learned a lot reading dictionaries. Dr Frederick C. Mish has learned a lot writing them. He is joint editorial director of the Merriam-Webster family of dictionaries and has taught me almost all I know about etymology, including the fact that it's the study of the history and origin of words and comes from the Greek *etymon* meaning "true meaning".

Over a cup of coffee he kindly explained that *coffee* comes from the Italian *caffe*, which derives from the Turkish word *kahve*, which in turn comes from the Arabic *quahwah*. He also revealed that *catsup* comes from the Malay word *kechap*, meaning "spiced fish sauce". *Bamboo* is also from a Malay word spelled *bambu*. From Tahitian we get *tatoo*, which means the same in Tahiti as it does at home. The Chinese gave us *tea*, and from the Persian comes *shawl*.

"Quite often," according to Dr Mish, "when the first settlers in a country found something new, they simply adopted the native word for it. When the first English settlers spotted what the Algonquian Indians called an *urahkun*, they took the Indian word and made it *raccoon*. In fact, the American Indian gave us such words as *persimmon, hickory, caucus* and many others."

Here are some more Mish marvels selected at random from the international melting pot of words. The word *goulash* is a good old Hungarian word, *gulyas,* meaning "herdsman's stew". The Finns invented the *sauna*, and we have their word for it. *Cashew* came from the Portuguese. *Pastrami* is from the Rumanian *pastrama* by way of Yiddish. And *whisky* is from the Irish Gaelic and Scottish Gaelic – of course!

Dorothy Lamour wore one and made it famous, and the word for *sarong* comes from the Malay *kain sarong*, meaning "a cloth sheath". *Shampoo* is from the Hindi; *molasses* from Portuguese; *hanker* probably from Flemish; and *boomerang* is a native name in Australia.

*Swastika* is not a German word, despite its having been made famous by Hitler. It is from Sanskrit. In fact, the sign itself is an old one and is found in many civilizations.

Our word *pal* is from the Romany *phal*, which means "brother" or "friend". Romany is the Indic language of the Gypsies. *Pariah* is from Tamil, in which language it literally means "drummer" and refers to a member of a low caste of southern India and Burma. We use the word to mean "outcast". *Kowtow* is from the Chinese and means, literally, "to bump the head".

The word *kosher* is from Yiddish and came in turn from Hebrew where it meant "fit, proper". The word *khaki* is from the Hindi and means "dust-coloured" in that language. *Mammoth* comes from the Russian word *mamont; thug* is from the Hindi word for thief; *sleigh* from the Dutch; and *assassin* from the Arabic *hashshashin*, which means "one addicted to hashish".

The word *penguin* may come from the Welsh *pen gwyn*, meaning "white head". *Pyjama* is from the Hindi, and *robot* from the Czech, meaning "work". The name for our old friend the chipanzee comes from a word in the Kongo dialect. And *taboo* comes from the Tonga Islands of the Southwest Pacific. In Tongan, *tabu* is something "charged with a dangerous supernatural power and forbidden to profane use".

## ORIGIN UNKNOWN

Dr Mish is a very clever man. He can give you the etymology of almost every word in the language, but some words have beaten him. And not just him. There are certain English words whose etymologies are unknown. Here are some of the words that have defeated the dictionary-makers. If you can shed any light on the mystery of their origin, Dr Mish would like to hear from you.

| | |
|---|---|
| *barf* | To vomit. |
| *boffin* | Scientific expert. |
| *bonkers* | Crazy, mad. |
| *clobber* | To pound, to defeat. |
| *codswallop* | Nonsense. |

| | |
|---|---|
| *dido* | Prank. |
| *dildo* | Penis substitute. |
| *dingleberry* | A shrub. |
| *faggot* | Homosexual. |
| *flub* | To botch. |
| *gizmo* | A gadget. |
| *gunnel* | A fish. |
| *hickey* | A device. |
| *hootenanny* | A gathering at which folk singers entertain. |
| *jive* | Swing music. |
| *kludge* | A system made up of components that are poorly matched. |
| *lobbygow* | An errand boy. |
| *lummox* | A clumsy person. |
| *lunker* | Something large of its kind. |
| *malarkey* | Bunkum. |
| *moola* | Money. |
| *pemoline* | A synthetic organic drug. |
| *pen* | A female swan. |
| *raddled* | Of unkempt or run-down appearance. |
| *rampike* | Erect, broken or dead tree. |
| *raunchy* | Lusty, sexual, earthy. |
| *rolamite* | A nearly frictionless elementary mechanism. |
| *scag* | Heroin. |
| *scrim* | A durable fabric. |
| *shandrydan* | Chaise with a hood. |
| *shim* | Thin piece of material. |
| *slather* | A great quantity. |
| *snaffle* | To obtain, especially by devious means. |
| *snitch* | To inform. |
| *toke* | A puff on a marijuana cigarette. |
| *trangam* | A trinket, or gimcrack. |
| *twerp* | A silly person. |
| *willies* | A fit of nervousness. |
| *zonked* | Being under the influence of alcohol. |

Of the words in the list I've long had a special sympathy for *twerp*, not for the obvious reason (thank you very much) but because, in 1969, when I became President of the Union at Oxford I was advised that my term of office coincided with the Golden Jubilee of the Presidency of one T.W. Earp of Exeter College and it was Earp who gave *twerp* to the language. According to one authority Earp inspired the word "because of the Goering-like wrath he kindled in the hearts of the rugger-playing stalwarts at Oxford ... by being the last, most charming and wittiest of the 'decadents'".

Just as it would be nice if the word *tip* was an acronym for To Insure Promptness and the word *posh* did derive from the expression Port Out Starboard Home (the preferred position for your cabin when sailing between Europe and India), it would be very gratifying if we could be sure that Earp really was the original *twerp*. Unfortunately, Dr Robert Burchfield, Editor of the *Oxford English Dictionary* and unparalleled force to be reckoned with on these matters, has his doubts. *Tip* and *posh* certainly aren't acronyms and poor Thomas Earp is an eponymist only if you're ready to give him the benefit of the doubt. Dr Burchfield isn't. His masterly *Supplement* to the *O.E.D.* (Volume IV, 1986) says simply that *twerp* is "of uncertain origin".

In fact *twerp* has taken quite a battering of late. In the spring of 1987 the word fell foul of the Speaker of the House of Commons who, during questions to the Secretary of State for the Environment, ruled: "I find the word *twerp* an inelegant parliamentary expression."

Happily there is at least one other former President of the Oxford Union who has given his name to the language and no dispute about it. By coincidence he was the very man T.W. Earp succeeded when he became President in 1919: Leslie Hore-Belisha. The *Belisha beacon*, "a post about seven feet high surmounted by a flashing amber-coloured globe and erected on the pavement at officially recognized pedestrian crossings of the highway", was introduced during Lord Hore-Belisha's time as Minister of Transport (1931–7).

# ANGELICAL ASPIRATES

Take a letter. Add another letter to make a word. Add a third letter to make a new word. Keep on adding letters and making longer words until you have to stop.

Here's how it's done:

| | |
|---|---|
| A | The first letter of the alphabet. |
| AN | The indefinite article. |
| ANG | The hairy part of an ear of barley. |
| ANGE | Trouble, affliction, anguish. |
| ANGEL | A celestial spirit. |
| ANGELI | A town in Sweden. |
| ANGELIC | Having the nature of an angel. |

| | |
|---|---|
| ANGELICA | A sweet dessert wine produced in California. |
| ANGELICAL | Having the nature of an angel. |
| ANGELICALS | Nuns of an extinct order established in Milan in 1530. |
| | |
| B | The second letter of the alphabet. |
| BU | An old Japanese gold coin. |
| BUT | A conjunction. |
| BUTT | A large cask. |
| BUTTE | An isolated hill or small mountain. |
| BUTTER | An important food. |
| BUTTERI | The surname of an Italian painter, 1540–1606. |
| BUTTERIN | A reformed spelling of *butterine*. |
| BUTTERINE | An imitation butter. |
| BUTTERINES | The plural of *butterine*. |
| BUTTERINESS | The quality of being buttery. |
| | |
| B | The second letter of the alphabet. |
| BI | Bisexual. |
| BIT | A piece. |
| BITT | A post on a ship's deck. |
| BITTE | A spelling of *bit* used in the fourteenth, fifteenth and sixteenth centuries. |
| BITTER | Sharp. |
| BITTERN | Any of various small and medium-sized herons. |
| BITTERNE | A seventeenth-century spelling of *bittern*. |
| BITTERNES | The plural of *bitterne*. |
| BITTERNESS | The quality of being bitter. |
| BITTERNESSE | An old spelling of *bitterness*. |
| BITTERNESSES | The plural of *bitterness*. |

Now try doing it the other way around, putting the new letter in front of the first letter.

| | |
|---|---|
| E | The fifth letter of the alphabet. |
| TE | A musical tone. |
| ATE | The past tense of *eat*. |
| RATE | A charge, payment, or price. |
| IRATE | Angry. |
| PIRATE | A robber on the high seas. |
| SPIRATE | Voiceless. |
| ASPIRATE | To pronounce with an *h* sound. |

Build this one on your own.

| | |
|---|---|
| — | The fifth letter of the alphabet. |
| — — | A musical tone. |
| — — — | The past tense of *eat*. |
| — — — — | A lock of hair. |
| — — — — — | Condition. |
| — — — — — — | A social or political class. |
| — — — — — — — | To state in a new form. |
| — — — — — — — — | In Roman and civil law, to perform. |

(See Answers, page 265.)

Over the page is another attractive arrangement of words. In the pattern on the left, the words *end* with all the different letters of the alphabet, progressing from *A* to *Z*, with their lengths varying from 1 to 13 letters and from 13 back to 1. In the pattern on the right, the words *begin* with all the different letters of the alphabet, progressing from *A* to *Z*, with their lengths varying from 1 to 13 and from 13 back to 1.

| | |
|---:|:---|
| A | A |
| OB | BE |
| SAC | CAT |
| LEAD | DIME |
| PLATE | ELECT |
| SCRUFF | FIERCE |
| MORNING | GROCERY |
| HAWFINCH | HORRIBLE |
| SPAGHETTI | INORGANIC |
| DARYAOGANJ | JUXTAPOSED |
| STICKLEBACK | KLEPTOMANIA |
| TETRARCHICAL | LIQUEFACTION |
| PARALLELOGRAM | MICROSCOPICAL |
| ACCREDITATION | NEFARIOUSNESS |
| WHILLABALLOO | OBSTREPEROUS |
| THUNDERCLAP | PALINDROMIC |
| QARAQALPAQ | QUADRUPLET |
| GODMOTHER | ROUGHNECK |
| SLOWNESS | SYMPHONY |
| CONTENT | THEREIN |
| BUREAU | UNDONE |
| SCLAV | VOICE |
| SLOW | WILD |
| BOX | XED |
| MY | YE |
| Z | Z |

*Daryaoganj* is the name of a town in India; *Qaraqalpaq* is a Turkic people of Central Asia; *Sclav* is a variant spelling of *Slav*, a person who speaks a Slavic language; and *xed* means "marked with a cross".

# B
## AA BAA BANANA!

There are numerous words that use a particular letter twice. For example, *there* has two *E*s, *numerous* has two *U*s, *particular* has two *A*s and two *R*s, and *letter* has two *E*s and two *T*s. Here is an A to Z of words in which the same letter appears twice.

| | | | | |
|---|---|---|---|---|
| a | *baa* | | n | *inn* |
| b | *ebb* | | o | *coo* |
| c | *cock* | | p | *pup* |
| d | *did* | | q | *quinquennium* |
| e | *bee* | | r | *err* |
| f | *off* | | s | *ass* |
| g | *gag* | | t | *tot* |
| h | *high* | | u | *usual* |

| i | iris | v | viva |
| j | jejune | w | wow |
| k | kick | x | executrix |
| l | all | y | yolky |
| m | mum | z | jazz |

A *quinquennium* is a five-year period; *viva* is an interjection of good will; and *executrix* is a female executor.

Compiling an A to Z of words in which the same letter appears three times is more difficult, but it can be done.

| a | banana | n | nanny |
| b | bobby | o | ovolo |
| c | coccyx | p | poppy |
| d | daddy | q | Qaraqalpaq |
| e | epee | r | error |
| f | fluff | s | sass |
| g | gaggle | t | tatty |
| h | heighth | u | unusual |
| i | iiwi | v | viva-voce |
| j | Jijjin | w | powwow |
| k | kakariki | x | hexahydroxycyclohexane |
| l | lull | y | syzygy |
| m | mummy | z | zizz |

*Heighth* is a dialectal spelling of *height; iiwi* is a brightly coloured Hawaiian bird; *Jijjin* is a town in Jordan; *kakariki* is both a parrakeet and a lizard from New Zealand; *Qarapalpaq* is a Turkic people of Central Asia; *hexahydroxycyclohexane* is a chemical, a member of the vitamin B complex, which is essential for life; and *zizz* is a whirring sound.

A complete A to Z of words in which the same letter is repeated four times is impossible. With *V* and *X* I failed, but I did my best with the rest.

| a | maharaja | n | nonunion |
| b | bubbybush | o | voodoo |

| | | | |
|---|---|---|---|
| c | *scacchic* | p | *whippersnapper* |
| d | *diddled* | q | *Qawiqsaqq* |
| e | *teepee* | r | *recurrer* |
| f | *riffraff* | s | *assess* |
| g | *gagging* | t | *statuette* |
| h | *high-thoughted* | u | *muumuu* |
| i | *visibility* | v | *???* |
| j | *jejunojejunostomy* | w | *wow-wow* |
| k | *kakkak* | x | *???* |
| l | *pellmell* | y | *fyyryryn* |
| m | *mummydom* | z | *razzmatazz* |

A *bubbybush* is another name for the strawberry shrub; *scacchic* means "relating to chess"; *high-thoughted* is merely having high thoughts; a *jejunojejunostomy* is the operative formation of a passage between two portions of the jejunum, part of the small intestine; a *kakkak* is a small bittern from the island of Guam; *Qawiqsaqq* is the náme of a particular bluff in Alaska; a *muumuu* is a loose dress worn mainly in Hawaii; a *wow-wow* is any of several gibbons; *fyyryryn* is a Middle English spelling of fire iron.

You won't be surprised to learn that I couldn't find words containing five *J*s, *Q*s, *V*s, or *X*s, but I managed the rest of the alphabet.

| | | | |
|---|---|---|---|
| a | *abracadabra* | n | *nonintervention* |
| b | *hubble-bubble* | o | *oronooko* |
| c | *circumcrescence* | p | *pepper-upper* |
| d | *fuddy-duddy* | q | *???* |
| e | *telemetered* | r | *terror-stirring* |
| f | *fluffy-ruffle* | s | *assesses* |
| g | *wiggle-waggling* | t | *totipotentiality* |
| h | *High-Churchmanship* | u | *Uburu-uku* |
| i | *illimitability* | v | *???* |
| j | *???* | w | *M'daywawkawntwawns* |
| k | *Kvikkjokk* | x | *???* |

| l | *lillypilly* | y | *gryffygryffygryffs* |
|---|---|---|---|
| m | *mmm'mm* | z | *Zzzzz* |

A *hubble-bubble* is a flurry of activity; a *circumcrescence* is a growing over; *fluffy-ruffle* is an adjective meaning with fluffy ruffled margins; *Kvikkjokk* is a town in Sweden; *lillypilly* is an Australian tree with hard, fine-grained wood; *mmm'mm* is sex appeal; *oronooko* is a type of tobacco; *totipotentiality* is a biological term, the capability of developing along any of the lines inherently possible; *Uburu-uku* is a place in Nigeria; *M'daywawkawntwawns* are Indians of the Dakota people, a name more frequently spelled *Mdewakantons; gryffygryffygryffs* comes from James Joyce's *Finnegans Wake*, about two-thirds of the way through chapter 11; and *Zzzzz* is the name of a wake-up service in Los Angeles.

## SEEING DOUBLE

Words in which the same letter appears twice and together are common enough. *Common*, with its double *M*, is one of them. Can you compile a list of twenty-six words in each of which a different letter of the alphabet appears twice and together? *JJ, QQ, XX*, and *YY* are the tough ones.

(See Answers, page 266.)

## THREE'S COMPANY

Finding words in which the same letters appear three, four, or more times in a row is a challenge, but I like to think I'm equal to it.

*Kaaawa* is the name of a town on the island of Oahu in Hawaii; and *Faaa* is the name of a settlement on the west coast of Tahiti.

*The Oxford English Dictionary* contains *weeest*, the superlative form of *wee*, in an illustrative quotation dating from 1878; the same dictionary also includes *seeer*, "one who sees".

*The American Thesaurus of Slang* contains the three words *pfff*, *pffft*, and *phffft*, all meaning "to go to ruin".

The exclamation *shhh*, requesting silence, seems common enough, but no dictionary actually deigns to list it. *Hmmm* does appear in dictionaries of slang and is an expression of pleasure or astonishment.

The straightforward *frillless*, without a frill, is given in *The Oxford English Dictionary*; and the similar *wallless* is in an earlier edition of the unabridged *Webster's*.

*Brrr* is expressive of shivering with cold or apprehension and appears in the 1972 Supplement to *The Oxford English Dictionary*.

There are several examples of three-S words. *The Oxford English Dictionary* contains *countessship*, *duchessship*, and *goddessship*, while its 1972 Supplement contains *bossship*. An earlier edition of *Webster's* gives both *headmistressship* and *patronessship*.

The *Oxford* offers two words with three *U*s: *vertuuus*, a fourteenth-century spelling of *virtuous*, and *uuula*, an early form of *uvula*.

*Bzzzbzzz* is given in *The American Thesaurus of Slang* as a synonym for *gossip*.

Four *A*s appear in *Aaaatamad*, the name of an unidentified town in ancient Palestine.

*Eeeeve* is the local name of the Hawaiian bird *iiwi*.

Four *O*s appear in the curious *Cookkoooose*, a name given to the tribes of the Kusan Indian family.

Four *S*s appear in the palindromic *esssse*, an old spelling of *ashes*, which is given as a main entry in *The Oxford English Dictionary*. And *zzzz* is given as a verb, "to snore", in *The American Thesaurus of Slang*.

*The American Thesaurus of Slang* also has *OOOOO* as an exclamation of surprise. In the eighteenth century, there was a British racehorse called *POTOOOOOOOO*. This was pronounced *potatoes*, made up from *pot* and *eight Os*.

The most extreme example to appear in print is in Philip Roth's best-selling *Portnoy's Complaint*. On the last page is a howl of anguish, represented by 231 consecutive *A*s, followed by four *H*s. Thus:

```
AAAAAAAAAAAAAAAAAAAAAAAAAAAAAAAAAAA-
AAAAAAAAAAAAAAAAAAAAAAAAAAAAAAAAAAA-
AAAAAAAAAAAAAAAAAAAAAAAAAAAAAAAAAAA-
AAAAAAAAAAAAAAAAAAAAAAAAAAAAAAAAAAA-
AAAAAAAAAAAAAAAAAAAAAAAAAAAAAAAAAAA-
AAAAAAAAAAAAAAAAAAAAAAAAAAAAAAAAAAA-
AAAAAAAAAAAAAAAAAAAAAHHHH
```

Beat that!

# CRITICAL CRITICS

The playwright Christopher Hampton once said: "Asking a working actor what he thinks about critics is like asking a lamp-post how it feels about dogs." It does happen and some playwrights have a ready answer. This was Brendan Behan's: "Critics are like eunuchs in a harem. They're there every night, they see it done every night, they see how it should be done every night, but they can't do it themselves."

The heyday of coruscating criticism in America was also the heyday of the Algonquin Round Table. The Table's leading lady, Dorothy Parker, managed to sum up one play in five words: "*House Beautiful* is play lousy." She was often as caustic but not always so concise. Here she is reviewing Margot Asquith's *Lay Sermons*:

In this book of essays, which has all the depth and glitter of a worn dime, the Countess walks right up to such subjects as Health, Human Nature, Fame, Character, Marriage, Politics, and Opportunities. A rather large order, you might say, but it leaves the lady with unturned hair. Successively, she knocks down and drags out each topic. And there is something vastly stirring in the way in which, no matter where she takes off from, she brings the discourse back to Margot Asquith. Such singleness of purpose is met but infrequently.

When she does get around to less personal matters, it turns out that her conclusions are soothingly far from startling. A compilation of her sentiments, suitably engraved upon a nice, big calendar, would make an ideal Christmas gift for your pastor, your dentist, or Junior's music teacher: Here, for instance, are a few ingots lifted from her golden treasury: "The artistic temperament has been known to land people in every kind of dilemma ..." "Pleasure will always make a stronger appeal than Wisdom ..." "It is only the fine natures that profit by Experience ..." "It is better to be a pioneer than a passenger, and best of all to try and create ..." "It is not only what you See but what you Feel that kindles appreciation and gives life to Beauty ..." "Quite apart from the question of sex, some of the greatest rascals have been loved ..." "I think it is a duty women owe not only to themselves, but to everyone else, to dress well."

The Thames, I hear, remains as damp as ever in the face of these observations.

Through the pages of *Lay Sermons* walk the great. I don't say that Margot Asquith actually permits us to rub elbows with them ourselves, but she willingly shows us her own elbow, which has been, so to say, honed on the mighty. "I remember President Wilson saying to me"; "John Addington Symonds once said to me"; "The Master of Balliol told me" – thus does she introduce her anecdotes. And you know those anecdotes that begin that way; me, I find them more efficacious than sheep-counting, rain on a tin roof, or alanol tablets. Just begin a story with such a phrase as "I remember Disraeli – poor old Dizzy! – once saying to me, in answer to my poke in the eye," and you will find me and Morpheus off in a corner, necking.

For brevity it would be hard to beat Alexander Woollcott's review of a show called *Wham!* His entire notice read "Ouch!"

It was Woollcott who, after yet another disappointing evening at the theatre, reported: "The audience strummed their catarrhs." And taking a designer to task in another play he singled out one piece of furniture and observed, "The chair . . . was upholstered in one of those flagrant chintzes, designed, apparently, by the art editor of a seed catalogue."

Heywood Broun was one of the more down-to-earth of the Algonquin set. He greeted a new arrival on Broadway with the sentence, "It opened at 8:40 sharp and closed at 10:40 dull." And when the English actor Montague Love appeared in New York, Broun summed up his performance with the observation, "Mr Love's idea of playing a he-man was to extend his chest three inches and then follow it slowly across the stage."

When Walter Kerr went to see *Hook and Ladder* he concluded: "It is the sort of play that gives failures a bad name." And on the opening night of a new comedy, George S. Kaufman reported: "There was laughter at the back of the theatre, leading to the belief that someone was telling jokes back there."

Not all the Algonquin set were negative. Franklin Pierce Adams even enthused over actress Minnie Maddern Fiske in verse:

Somewords she runstogether,

Some others are distinctly stated.

Somecometoofast and

    s o m e t o o s l o w

And some are $sy^n c_o p^a ted$.

And yet no voice—I am sincere—

Exists that I prefer to hear.

He was less charitable when he saw Helen Hayes as Cleopatra in Bernard Shaw's play *Caesar and Cleopatra* in 1925. In his review Adams remarked that it seemed as if the Egyptian queen was suffering from "Fallen archness".

And in any Hall of Fame for acid criticism, there has to be a special place for James Agee's verdict on the movie *Random Harvest*: "I would like to recommend this film to those who can stay interested in Ronald Colman's amnesia for two hours and who could with pleasure eat a bowl of Yardley's shaving soap before breakfast."

# D
## ICTIONARY WITH A DIFFERENCE

### Bierce My Heart

A cynic is a blackguard who sees things as they are, and not as they ought to be.

So said Ambrose Gwinnet Bierce, a brilliant blackguard and a considerable wit, who was born on June 24th 1842 in Meigs County, Ohio. He was the son of a farmer and, since he never went to school, what education he got came from reading his father's books. When he left home he went to work for the Mint in San Francisco and began writing articles for local weeklies. In 1871 his first short story – "The Haunted Valley" – was published. On Christmas Day of that year he married and sailed for England, where he joined the staff of the journal *Fun* and began publishing humorous writings.

He was a very funny writer – a satirist in the tradition of Mark Twain – but not a happy man. In 1913, at the age of seventy-one, he left for Mexico "with a pretty definite purpose, which, however, is not at present disclosable". He was never heard from again, but his memorial remains in the form of his extraordinary *Devil's Dictionary*, a unique volume addressed to those "enlightened souls who prefer dry wines to sweet, sense to sentiment, and wit to humour".

Here are ten typical definitions from the prince of cynical lexicographers:

*Altar* n. They stood before the altar and supplied/ the fire themselves in which their fat was fried.

*Brain*, n. An apparatus with which we think that we think.

*Cannon*, n. An instrument employed in the rectification of national boundaries.

*Debauchee*, n. One who has so earnestly pursued pleasure that he has had the misfortune to overtake it.

*Faith*, n. Belief without evidence in what is told by one who speaks without knowledge, of things without parallel.

*Genealogy*, n. An account of one's descent from a man who did not particularly care to trace his own.

*Marriage*, n. The state or condition of a community consisting of a master, a mistress and two slaves, making in all two.

*Patience*, n. A minor form of despair, disguised as a virtue.

*Philanthropist*, n. A rich (and usually bald) old gentleman who has trained himself to grin while his conscience is picking his pocket.

*Prejudice*, n. A vagrant opinion without visible means of support.

## BOWKER'S DOZEN

Gordon Bowker is a modern writer who has inherited Bierce's mantle of cynicism. Bowker's approach and tone are different from Bierce's, but some of his definitions are equally telling.

*advertise*  A form of prestidigitating by means of which a conjuror induces his audience to pick its own pocket under the impression that it is picking someone else's.

*bigamy*  A slip of the memory and the pen in the presence of the marriage register under the influence of matrimony.

*body-builder*   One who is fit for nothing.

*celibate*   A member of a union opposed to the union of members.

*divorce*   The stage of marriage at which sanity prevails.

*drunk*   A miracle worker who, while being unable to walk on water, is frequently to be seen staggering on whisky.

*elitist*   A humanist so inspired by the principle of equality that he strives to ensure that as many people as possible are equally deprived.

*epitaph*   An irritating reminder that someone else always has the last word.

*freeloading*   A quality of generosity that impels one human being to take the weight off another human being's feet by the simple device of taking the food off his plate.

*gay*   To be thoroughly bent on pleasure.

*hangover*   The mourning after the night before.

*hooker*   A fisher of men.

*horoscope*   A tale told by an idiot and believed by a fool.

*know-all*   A benevolent ignoramus whose poverty of knowledge does not inhibit his generosity of mouth.

*libel*   A slip of the pen frequently precipitating a slip of the bank balance.

*marxist*   A prophet of doom who predicts the doom of pro it.

*moonie*   A lune with a view.

*orgy*   A coming together of like-minded people.

*pathologist*   One who carves a good living out of a bad death.

*psychiatry*   The art of claiming to be able to cure those who are strung up practised by one who deserves to be.

*race course*   Place where the rich get richer and the poor get excited.

*salesman*   A contortionist who puts his foot in your door, his tongue in your ear and his hand in your pocket while peddling.

*shop steward*   A benevolent soul who, being blind himself, is nevertheless prepared to lead others who are similarly stricken.

*thief*   A businessman who does not issue receipts.

*tight*   A condition of legless man and a garment of one-legged woman.

*toy pistol*   A gun-of-a-son.

# E ARTHQUAKE

Standing in line waiting to see the movie *Earthquake*, my verbivore friend Darryl Francis asked me: "How many other words end in *-quake*?"

Instantly I erupted with *moonquake* and *seaquake*, but that was it.

After the film I went home to consult *Webster's New International Dictionary* (Second Edition) and came up with a total of nine.

| | |
|---|---|
| *cowquake* | Any of several grasses. |
| *earthquake* | A trembling of the earth. |
| *heartquake* | Fear or trepidation (an anagram of *earthquake*). |
| *icequake* | The crash attending the breaking up of ice masses. |
| *seaquake* | A seismic disturbance at sea. |

| | |
|---|---|
| *statequake* | A humorous term for a political upheaval in a state. |
| *sunquake* | A solar phenomenon like an earthquake. |
| *waterquake* | A disturbance of water by seismic action. |
| *worldquake* | A quake that shakes or affects the entire world. |

Recuperating from the seismic shock of discovering that *cowquake* is a type of grass and not a bovine upheaval, I turned to the current unabridged *Webster's* and found these two *-quake* words:

| | |
|---|---|
| *aquake* | Quaking. |
| *moonquake* | An agitation of the moon's surface that is analogous to a terrestrial earthquake. |

Then I found that the 1976 Supplement to the *Oxford English Dictionary* has this to offer:

| | |
|---|---|
| *mirthquake* | An entertainment that excites convulsive mirth. |

*A Dictionary of New English* (by Barnhart, Steinmetz, and Barnhart) gave me a couple more:

| | |
|---|---|
| *starquake* | A series of rapid changes in the shape of a star or in the distribution of its matter. |
| *youthquake* | The worldwide agitation caused by student uprisings and other expressions of rebellion among youth during the 1960s and 1970s. |

And I was delighted to discover that in their *Second Barnhart Dictionary of New English*, the authors have uncovered an extra three:

| | |
|---|---|
| *corequake* | A violent structural disruption in the core of a planet or star. |
| *crustquake* | A violent structural disruption in the crust of a planet or star. |
| *Marsquake* | A major seismic disturbance on the planet Mars. |

When I got to seventeen *-quake* words I thought I'd reached the limit, but then Darryl sent me two press cuttings. The first was from *Newsweek* and said of a particular earthquake: "It was not a superquake as earth tremors go." The other press report appeared in *The Times* and gave names to the quakes occurring on the planets within the solar system:

Marsquakes will be the first, then venusquakes and mercuryquakes, jupiterquakes, saturnquakes, uranusquakes, neptunequakes and plutoquakes. . . . And then the moons of these planets, Mars giving phobosquakes and deimosquakes, and Jupiter with its 12 satellites.

That makes a grand total of twenty-seven *quake* words. If you come across any others, do let me know. The effect could be cataclysmic.

# FLEXILOQUENTLY SPEAKING

To me *flexiloquent* is one of the loveliest words in the English language, but back in 1678 a man called Phillips tried to get it banned. In his treatise *New World of Words* Phillips gave a list of words "to be used warily ... or totally to be rejected as barbarous and illegally compounded or derived". These he regarded as "most notorious":

| | |
|---|---|
| acetologous | logographer |
| acercecomie | lubidinity |
| alebromancy | lubrefaction |
| ambilogie | luctisonant |
| anopsie | miniography |
| aurigraphy | nihilification |
| circumbilivagination | nugipolyloquous |

clemsonize
colligence
comprint
cynarctomachy
effigiate
essentificate
fallaciloquent
flexiloquent
helisphaerical
hierogram
holographical
homologation
horripilation
humidiferous
illiquation
importous
imprescriptible
incommiscibility
indign
inimical

nugisonant
olfact
onologie
parvipension
plastography
plausidical
quadrigamist
quadrisyllabous
repatriation
scelestick
solisequious
superficialize
syllabize
synscentrick
transpeciation
tristitiation
ultimity
vaginipennous
viscated
vulpinarity

Fortunately some of the words that offended Phillips have survived, among them:

agonize
autograph
bibliography
cacophony
euthanasia

ferocious
hagiography
misanthropist
misogynist

*Flexiloquent*, meaning "speaking persuasively", definitely deserves to survive, and I am not alone in wanting to see (and hear) it brought back into general use.

Championing its cause, verbivore and crossword guru Roger Millington has launched an international campaign known as SUFF (Speak Up for Flexiloquent) on the grounds that we would all be better occupied reviving beautiful old words like *flexiloquent* than creating horrific new words and phrases like these:

| | |
|---|---|
| *kidvid* | Children's television. |
| *sciencing out* | Removing defects from a product by scientific research. |
| *sod poodles* | Gun enthusiasts' name for prairie dogs. |
| *wetware* | Computer jargon for the human brain. |

## FLEXILOQUENT FAVOURITES

A few years ago, on the night of April 3rd-4th 1982, I made my way into the *Guiness Book of Records* when I got up and gave the longest-ever after-dinner speech. I talked nonstop for twelve and a half hours. It wasn't too difficult because I come from a family known for its verbosity.

As children my three sisters, my brother, and I were positively encouraged to speak in public by being taught a multitude of wonderful word games. Played often enough, they should help anyone speak with greater quick-wittedness, clarity, fluency, and flexiloquence.

Here are half-a-dozen Brandreth family favourites.

## COFFEEPOT

One of the players must block his ears while all the others choose a secret verb. When the verb's been chosen, the victim unblocks his ears and begins to question the others, substituting the word *coffeepot* for the mysterious verb. "How often do you coffeepot?" might be one question. "Can the over-eighties coffeepot with ease?" might be another. The victim is allowed ten questions, to which he must be given sensible replies and after which he must guess the identity of the secret verb. If he guesses correctly he gains a point and another player becomes the victim. The first player to score five points is the winner.

## JUST A MINUTE

Players take it in turn to talk on a set subject for just a minute. They start with ten points apiece and when they have been talking for sixty seconds, without hesitating, repeating themselves, or deviating from the subject, they are awarded a further five points. However, if they *are* guilty of hesitation, repetition, or deviation they *lose* two points. Before the game starts an impartial observer should be asked to choose the subjects, impose the penalties, and keep the score.

The more ridiculous the phrases the more entertaining the sixty seconds become. Almost anyone can talk about "Having a bath" for just a minute, but it is not so easy to keep going with topics like "Rat-catching in Oswego" and "I was a teenage taxidermist".

This, of course, is a brilliantly successful radio game, devised by Ian Messiter, and a firm favourite with the BBC for more than two decades.

## MESSING ABOUT IN QUOTES

One player comes up with a well-known phrase or quotation or cliché, and the other player has to suggest who might have said it. The players then swap roles. Nobody is awarded any points, penalties, or prizes, but with quick-witted players the game can be a joy. To set you going, who said, "Thank God it's Friday"? Why, Robinson Crusoe, of course!

## WHAT'S THE PROVERB

A victim is chosen and asked to cover his ears and eyes while the other players choose a secret proverb. They then tell the victim how many words the proverb contains, and he asks them each a question in an attempt to arrive at the proverb's identity. The victim gets his clues because the first player must include the first word of the proverb in his answer, the second player the second, the third the third, and so on until all the words in the proverb have been accounted for.

With "Too many cooks spoil the broth" as the secret proverb, the questioning might go something like this:

| | |
|---|---|
| QUESTION: | Does this proverb express a basic truth about life? |
| ANSWER: | Yes, definitely. If anything, I'd say it's almost *too* true. |
| QUESTION: | Has it anything to do with love? |
| ANSWER: | *Many* proverbs have, but this one hasn't. |
| QUESTION: | Is it a sort of warning? |
| ANSWER: | You mean like "He who *cooks* the books ends up in jail"? Yes, I'd say it is. |
| QUESTION: | Is it a proverb about domestic life? |
| ANSWER: | Oh, I think it'd *spoil* the game if I gave you a straight answer to that. |
| QUESTION: | Is it an old proverb? |
| ANSWER: | *The* oldest I know. |
| QUESTION: | When did you first hear it? |
| ANSWER: | Years ago, when I was on holiday in Scotland, supping on *broth* and homemade bread, I was told it by a crofter's wife. |

The questioner is allowed two questions for every word in the proverb and scores five points if he guesses it correctly when he has asked his allotted questions. At the end of a set number of rounds, the player with the highest score is the winner.

## WORD LIGHTNING

The leader chooses a victim and gives him a letter. The hapless victim then has sixty seconds in which to rattle off as many words as he can that begin with the chosen letter. The leader keeps count. When all the players have been given a letter and a minute to do their best in, the player with the highest word count is the winner.

## WORD ORDER

The first player calls out a word at random, the second player follows with another word suggested by the first word, the third player with another suggested by the second, and so on around the group. If the first word were *apple*, it might be followed by *pie, sky, blue, colour, television, set, match, stick, cane, sugar,* and so on.

After a few rounds the first player suddenly shouts "Reverse order!" at which point the last player to speak must remember the word before his and all the words are repeated around the group in the reverse order – from *sugar* to *cane* to *stick* to *match* to *set* to *television* to *colour* to *blue* to *sky* to *pie* to *apple*.

Anyone hesitating, getting the words in the wrong order, or forgetting a word loses a life. The player who has lost the least lives after five rounds is the winner.

# G IRL TALK

Who said it?

1 I don't mind living in a man's world as long as I can be a woman in it.
*Brigitte Bardot or Marilyn Monroe?*

2 Whether women are better than men I cannot say – but I can say they are certainly no worse.
*Golda Meir or Indira Gandhi?*

3 Women should remain at home, sit still, keep house, and bear and bring up children.
*Martin Luther or Martin Luther King?*

4 Men seldom make passes at a girl who surpasses.
*Franklin P. Jones or Dorothy Parker?*

5 Once made equal to man, woman becomes his superior.
*Socrates or Germaine Greer?*

6 There are no woman composers, never have been and possibly never will be.
*Thomas Beecham or Thea Musgrave?*

7 Despite my thirty years of research into the feminine soul, I have not yet been able to answer ... the great question that has never been answered: What does a woman want?
*Sigmund Freud or Woody Allen?*

8 The only question left to be settled now is, are women persons?
*Twiggy or Susan B. Anthony?*

9 Well, it's hard for a mere man to believe that woman doesn't have equal rights.
*Dwight D. Eisenhower or Norman Mailer?*

10 But if God had wanted us to think with our wombs, why did He give us a brain?
*Erica Jong or Clare Boothe Luce?*

11 A suburban mother's role is to deliver children obstetrically once, and by car forever after.
*Peter de Vries or Dr Benjamin Spock?*

12 When men reach their sixties and retire, they go to pieces. Women just go right on cooking.
*Gail Sheehy or Betty Friedan?*

13 Woman's virtue is man's greatest invention.
*Oscar Wilde or Cornelia Otis Skinner?*

14 Fighting is essentially a masculine idea; a woman's weapon is her tongue.
*Hermione Gingold or Nancy Reagan?*

15 I'm a revolutionary – a revolutionary woman!
*Mae West or Jane Fonda?*

16 God made man, and then said I can do better than that and made woman.
*Adela Rogers St. John or Billy Graham?*

17 I feel very angry when I think of brilliant, or even interesting women whose minds are wasted on a home. Better have an affair. It isn't so permanent and you keep your job.
*John Kenneth Galbraith or Cecil Parkinson?*

18 There are two kinds of women: those who want power in the world, and those who want power in bed.
*Jacqueline Kennedy Onassis or Zsa Zsa Gabor?*

19 No one is born a woman.
*Simone de Beauvoir or April Ashley?*

20 Women who insist upon having the same options as men would do well to consider the option of being the strong silent type.
*Fran Lebowitz or Ruby Wax?*

(See Answers, page 266.)

## MS-ELLANEOUS

If the US Weather Bureau can break the habit of a lifetime and give hurricanes men's names, I think the rest of us should do our best to avoid sexist language as well. It's ridiculous – and unnecessary – as these recent examples prove:

"The annual exhibition of the Society of Craftsmen – which includes women artists as well – opens on Thursday . . ."

" . . . in terms even a housewife can understand."

"The Pap test, which has greatly reduced mortality from uterine cancer, is a boon to mankind."

"Judy Chicago will have her third one-man show this summer."

"It's the great secret of doctors, known only to their wives, that most ailments get better by themselves."

"What earthly purpose is served by tying a knot around your neck every day just so you can look like every other member of the species?"

"The average person (in one year) finds it no problem at all to have three head colds, one sunburn, an attack of athlete's foot, twenty headaches, three hangovers, and five temper tantrums with adolescent children and still get in his sixty-one hours of shaving."

I know I should try to use nonsexist English and I do. But I don't know whether to use Ms instead of Miss and Mrs. Opinions are still sharply divided:

> When you call me Miss or Mrs
> You invade my private life,
> For it's not the public's business
> If I am, or was, a wife.

Others feel differently:

> In typing *Ms* for *Mrs*
> Your typewriter has slipped.
> I am a wife and mother,
> And not a manuscript.

Given that we all have first names, do we need titles at all?
When you meet me in the street, you needn't bother with Mr.
Just call me Gyles.

# H IGH AND MIGHTY

## TALK TALL

You will be familiar with tall stories, but you may not know about tall *words*. Known as extenders, they are the ones in which all the letters are written with extensions either above or below the line. In handwriting and lowercase type, the extenders are *b, d, f, g, h, i, j, k, l, p, q, t*, and *y*. *Light* and *filthy* are good examples of words made up exclusively of extenders. If you want to talk tall, make sure your conversation is peppered with tall words.

Here is a concise vocabulary of extenders for you to master:

*2 letters*: by, hi, id, if, it

*3 letters*: bib, bid, bit, did, dig, dip, fib, fig, fit, fly, gig, hid, hip, hit, ilk, ill, jib, kid, kip, kit, lid, lip, lit, pig, pip, pit, ply, thy, tip, tit

*4 letters*: bilk, bill, fill, flip, flit, gift, gild, glib, high, hill, hilt, idly, jilt, kill, kilt, lift, lilt, lily, pill, pith, tidy, til!

*5 letters*: biddy, billy, bitty, digit, ditty, fifth, fifty, fight, filth, giddy, glyph, hilly, idyll, kitty, light, piggy, pithy, thigh, tight

*6 letters*: blight, fillip, flight, giggly, glibly, highly, plight, tidbit

The English language boasts hundreds of tall two-to-six-letter words but not many with seven letters or more. Here is the complete range:

*7 letters*: bifidly, biggity, blighty, diglyph, fifthly, fittily, flighty, lightly, lithify, tightly, tiptilt

*8 letters*: bifidity, filthify, libidibi, philippi

*9 letters*: flightily, lilipilly

*10 letters*: lillypilly

Anthropologists reckon that the world's tallest people are Australians, so it's appropriate that *lillypilly*, the world's longest tallest word, should turn out to be a tall Australian tree with hard, fine-grained wood.

## WEIGHTY WORDS

If each letter of the alphabet is given a weight – whether it's pounds, ounces, or kilograms – then every word in the language has a weight equal to the sum of the weights of the individual letters. Naturally the letter *A* should be given a weight of one unit, *B* two units, and so on through the alphabet, ending up with *Z* having a weight of twenty-six units.

Obviously the lightest one-letter word is going to be the indefinite article *A*, but what is the lightest two-letter word? And what about longer words? I decided to search for the lightest words of all lengths up to fifteen letters. For each word in my list, I've given the total weight, the average weight per letter, and a brief definition. As might be expected, the average letter weight slowly increases with the length of the word, but there are occasional reversals.

*aa*                 (total weight = 2; average weight = 1.00) a type of volcanic lava.

| | |
|---|---|
| *baa* | (4 and 1.33) a sheep's bleat. |
| *abba* | (6 and 1.50) a coarse fabric woven in the Middle East from wool. |
| *caaba* | (8 and 1.60) relating to the Islamic shrine at Mecca. |
| *bacaba* | (10 and 1.67) a palm, the fruits of which yield an oil used in soap manufacture. |
| *cachaca* | (20 and 2.86) white rum. |
| *Fabaceae* | (24 and 3.00) a family of plants that includes peas, beans, and various woody plants with pea-like flowers. |
| *abdicable* | (39 and 4.33) able to abdicate. |
| *Galacaceae* | (39 and 3.90) a family of herbs and shrubs. |
| *cabbagehead* | (39 and 3.55) a thick-witted person. |
| *Baba-Abdallah* | (47 and 3.92) a character in *The Arabian Nights*. |
| *cabbageheaded* | (48 and 3.69) stupid. |
| *Hamamelidaceae* | (81 and 5.79) a family of shrubs and trees comprising the witch hazels and related plants. |
| *Coleochaetaceae* | (102 and 6.80) a family of green algae. |

The fourteen-letter specimen, *Hamamelidaceae*, is additionally interesting since it is the longest known word with all of its letters coming from the first half of the alphabet, *A* to *M*.

Having chased up fifteen lightweight words, I could hardly ignore the challenge of searching for fifteen heavy-weight words – the words that have the greatest weights for each of the lengths up to fifteen letters. Here they are:

| | |
|---|---|
| *z* | (total weight = 26; average weight = 26) something having the shape of the letter *z*. |
| *wy* | (48 and 24.00) something having the shape of the letter *y*. |
| *zuz* | (73 and 24.33) a silver coin of ancient Palestine. |
| *zu-zu* | (94 and 23.50) a soldier in the American Civil War. |
| *wuzzy* | (121 and 24.20) drunk. |

| | |
|---|---|
| *xystus* | (128 and 21.33) a tree-lined walk. |
| *Zyzomys* | (149 and 21.29) a genus of small Australian rodents. |
| *untrusty* | (158 and 19.75) not to be trusted. |
| *Zorotypus* | (175 and 19.44) a genus of insects. |
| *tuzzymuzzy* | (229 and 22.90) a garland of flowers. |
| *trustworthy* | (207 and 18.82) worthy of confidence. |
| *untumultuous* | (218 and 18.17) not turbulent. |
| *untrustworthy* | (242 and 18.61) not worthy of confidence. |
| *tumultuousness* | (240 and 17.14) commotion. |
| *untrustworthily* | (263 and 17.53) not in a trustworthy manner. |

# I
## NTERNATIONAL SCRABBLE

I was in prison when I decided to launch Britain's National Scrabble Championships.

I wasn't an inmate, you understand. I was just visiting – doing research for a book about prisons – and I happened to notice a couple of jailbirds playing the game. I already knew that Scrabble was the Royal Family's favourite board game, but I hadn't realized before that its popularity was so universal: that it could delight not just Her Majesty but even those detained in her prisons at her pleasure. There and then I decided that any game that had such a breadth of appeal had to have its own national tournament.

Of the labels that have been attached to me since I launched the first Scrabble Championship back in 1971 – "Scrabble King", "Scrabble Guru", "Mr Scrabble" – the one I treasure most appeared in a newspaper noted for its inspired misprints. "Mr Gyles Brandreth," it said, 'is the founder and organiser of the National Rabble Championships."

Let me say at once that there are no more civilized people on the planet than Scrabble players, but it can't be denied that passions *do* get aroused from time to time. As the poet – in this case, Scrabble laureate Robin Anderson – puts it so perfectly in his "Ode to Scrabble":

> Where double beats treble but triple beats all
> But you may have to settle for nothing at all
> And chuck in your letters
> And grope for their betters
> And bring out a handful still worse than before:
> Where your noun if deemed proper
> Will bring you a cropper
> And a cheat is worth more than playing fair
> Where with just one *E* more
> You've a staggering score
> And your word may be rude – you don't care:
> You are plotting and scheming, quixotically dreaming
> Of clearing your tray and going out
> But the next player's eyed
> The place you had espied
> And your staggering score's up the spout;
> So you spring from your chair
> Raise the board in the air
> And smash it down hard round his ears –
> Other players are crying
> The letters are flying:
> You're charged and end up with three years
> If your nerves are not icy, your temper is dicey,
> When losing, you tear out your hair;
> If you can't keep your cool
> Then follow the rule –
> When you dabble with Scrabble, beware!

Among the countries that hold national Scrabble championships in English are Singapore and the United Kingdom.

Both use *Chambers Twentieth Century Dictionary* as their reference when a word is in dispute, though each places different limitations upon the type of word permitted. For example, Scottish words are not valid in Singapore although they frequently appear on UK Scrabble boards. Some of these same words of Scottish origin *are* valid in the United States provided that they also appear in *The Official Scrabble Players Dictionary*. The *OSPD* is the reference used in official American competitions with the result that the United Kingdom and the United States will, sometimes, be at variance over which words are or are not valid for competitive Scrabble.

To illustrate that often-entertaining difference, here are half a dozen puzzles based upon various games of Scrabble at various stages in play. At the point at which the puzzle begins, all words on the board are valid in both the United Kingdom and the United States and you are given a rack of seven tiles to play.

It's your move and the challenge is to use your tiles to achieve the highest possible score – using either British words or American words or both.

Puzzles begin on the following page.

AEEGLRS

AEELRST

AADOPRX

OGJOQWZ

AAIJNRZ

**ABGILOO**

(NOTE: the *G* in AMBLING is a blank tile.)

(See Answers, page 267.)

# J ARGON FOR BEGINNERS

### BUREAUCRATESE

A few years ago a White House lawyer apologized to President Carter for producing an incomprehensible piece of legalese and then said: "I see your point, Mr President. I had better laymanize the whole thing."

More recently Malcolm Baldridge, President Reagan's Secretary for Commerce, admonished his staff for their over-blown use of English. Secretary Baldridge wanted his officials to adopt a concise style "halfway between Zane Grey and Ernest Hemingway".

The prospect of government documents written in a kind of English that's both Grey and Earnest may not be that appetizing, but it can only be an improvement on the bureaucratese that all too often is the order of the day. At this moment in time – if you'll pardon the expression – on both sides of the Atlantic we are still being fed incomprehensible gobbledygook like this:

> Any employee whose current salary rate exceeds the new top of the salary range for his or her classification will not be eligible for the general increase unless the new top of the salary range for his or her classification exceeds the employee's current salary rate.

> Component corporations of component corporations – If a corporation is a component corporation of an acquiring corporation, under subsection (b) or under this subsection, it shall (except for the purposes of section 742d and section 743a) also be a component corporation of the corporation of which such acquiring corporation is a component corporation.

> Apparatus for removing casings from sausages and the like (US Patent No. 2,673,646)
> In a sausage-skinning machine, means for rotating a sausage about its longitudinal axis, means for simultaneously holding a part of the skin against rotative movement with the sausage to cause said skin to be torn off said sausage circumferentially, and means for simultaneously removing said sausage endwise with respect to said holding means, said rotating, holding and moving means being operatively related to one another to cause said skin to be torn off and stripped from the sausage helically.

The Occupational and Safety Health Administration Rulebook defines "an exit" as:

> ...that portion of a means of egress which is separated from all other spaces of the building or structure by construction or equipment as required in this subpart to provide a protected way of travel to the exit discharge.

And "a means of egress" as:

> ...a continuous and unobstructed way of exit travel from any point in the building or structure to a public way and consists of three separate and distinct parts: the way of exit access, the exit and the way of exit discharge.

## COMMERCIALESE

Understanding the jargon of the worlds of business and commerce isn't easy, but if you want to get to the top you need to know what your colleagues – and your rivals – are talking about. To help you gain a better understanding of contemporary commercialese, here are edited highlights from Paul Dickson's penetrating glossary of useful words and phrases:

*Activate.* To make carbons and add more names to the memo.

*Advanced design.* Beyond the comprehension of the ad agency's copywriters.

*All new.* Parts not interchangeable with existing models.

*Approved, subject to comment.* Redraw the damned thing.

*Automatic.* That which you can't repair yourself.

*Channels.* The trail left by interoffice memos.

*Clarify, to.* To fill in the background with so many details that the foreground goes underground.

*Confidential memorandum.* No time to photocopy for the whole office.

*Consultant.* Someone who borrows your watch to tell you what time it is – then walks away with the watch.

*Coordinator.* The person who has a desk between two expediters (see *expedite.*)

*Developed after years of intensive research.* Discovered by accident.

*Expedite.* To confound confusion with commotion.

*Forwarded for your consideration.* You hold the bag for a while.

*Give someone the picture, to.* To make a long, confused, and inaccurate statement to a newcomer.

*Give us the benefit of your present thinking.* We'll listen to what you have to say as long as it doesn't interfere with what we've already decided to do.

*In conference.* Nobody can find him/her.

*In due course.* Never.

*Infrastructure.* (1) The structure within an infra. (2) The structure outside the infra. (3) A building with built-in infras.

*It is in process.* So wrapped up in red tape that the situation is almost hopeless.

*Let's get together on this.* I'm assuming you're as confused as I am.

*Note and initial.* Let's spread the responsibility for this.

*Policy.* We can hide behind this.

*See me.* Come down to my office, I'm lonely.

*Sources.* Reliable source – the person you just met. Informed source – the person who told the person you just met. Unimpeachable source – the person who started the rumour originally.

*Top priority.* It may be idiotic, but the boss wants it.

*Under active consideration.* We're looking in the files for it.

*We are making a survey.* We need more time to think of an answer.

*We will look into it.* By the time the wheel makes a full turn, we assume you will have forgotten about it too.

# K ARAT SOUP

## CHAUVINISM FOR BEGINNERS

Sometimes the English used by English-speaking people makes me despair. Then I go abroad and discover the English used by non-English-speaking people is even worse. On my travels I have collected examples of "foreigners' English" from all over the world. Here are the best – or worst:

> By order of the police, one obliges the frequenters of the Camping to are wearing bath-costumes that are not giving offence to the morals. (Notice in campsite in Italy)

> It is forbidden to steal hotel towels please. If you are not to do such is please not to read notis. (Notice in Tokyo hotel)

> Persons are requested not to occupy seats in this café without consummation. (Notice in French café)

In case of fire please do your utmost to alarm the hall porter. (Notice in Austrian hotel)

Visitors are requested not to throw coffee or other matter into the basin. Why else it stuffs the place inconvenient for the other world. (Notice in an Italian hotel)

## WHAT YOU MUST NOT DO

To walk around alone or in groups, in an inadequate form and adapting attitudes that denote a personal bad state, to offend the elemental conduct.

To make noises and scandals in the sight of the public and establishments.

Sit down or lie down in sight of the public, to obstruct the freedom of the people.

Utilizing ponds, fountains, for personal use.

To break or tear objects in the sight of the public or crowded places.

To utilize percussion instruments after midnight. (Notice from festival in Pamplona, Spain)

Gerona. Here is a name and a symbol. A name set in the tentacles of Empire. Of aristocratic craddle. Old and fruitful savour, speaking about daring legions, unfinishing ways, aqueducts, warlike marching and toges. Gerona was promise and reality. Promise because upon it would fall the evangelic seed of the mustard, not because less strong in aborescence and the fruit. (From a guidebook to Gerona, Spain)

To remember of this period are the failed lading of the French revolutionaries on the northern coast of the island (1793), the uprising of 1795, the consequent march of the judge C. M. Angioi on Cagliari, thwarted off Oristano in 1796 and the attempt also fruitless of the notary Cilocca in 1802. (From a guidebook to Sardinia)

Although every possible care has been taken, I do not accept responsibility for inoccurancies. (From a guidebook to Malta)

## TRANSLATION PLEASE

Foreigners' English may be bad at times, but the way English-speaking people speak other languages is invariably worse. Here is a glossary of words and phrases in French, German, Arabic, Spanish, Italian, and Latin, with a selection of very English translations . . .

| | |
|---|---|
| *abito* | A piece of. |
| *ahorros* | Four-legged animal used for racing. |
| *à la carte* | Served from the trolley. |
| *à la russe* | In a hurry. |
| *Angebot* | To wait, loiter. |
| *apenas* | Joy, pleasure. |
| *apéritif* | Dentures. |
| *arriba* | Large stream. |
| *Auspuff* | Cobweb duster. |
| *bacchich* | Backache. |
| *bagatelle* | Talkative females |
| *baroque* | Short of money. |
| *beau geste* | Big joke. |
| *bonis avibus* | Free ride on public transport. |
| *billet* | Academic qualification. |
| *bord de la route* | Soliciting hitchhiker. |
| *brouhaha* | French joy of cooking. |
| *brefs* | Pants. |
| *café Nero* | Coffee served with brandy on the surface. |
| *campagna* | Italian girlfriend. |
| *ça ne fait rien* | Good weather. |
| *carte blanche* | Hospital trolley. |
| *château* | French conversation. |
| *cortège* | Small house in the country. |
| *coup de cheveaux* | Horse race. |
| *crèche* | Sound of breaking crockery. |
| *cul-de-sac* | Out of the bag. |

| | |
|---|---|
| *damnosa* | Very inquisitive. |
| *de gustibus* | Very windy. |
| *déjeuner* | Travel. |
| *de mal en pis* | Urgent need to pass water. |
| *de optimo maximo* | Very good eyesight. |
| *déshabiller* | To kick the habit. |
| *émeraudes* | Piles. |
| *en ami* | Hostile person. |
| *esprit de corps* | Liquor served in military messes. |
| *extrados* | More, please. |
| *farceur* | Comic play. |
| *farci* | Farce. |
| *fiasco* | Italian wine bottle. |
| *flèche* | Skin. |
| *fruits de mer* | Sea weed. |
| *grande dame* | Fat lady. |
| *grand prix* | Large reward. |
| *hasta la vista* | You have nice views. |
| *homme d'affaires* | Libertine. |
| *hors de combat* | Dog fight. |
| *imo pectore* | He kissed her. |
| *in toto* | Wearing a ballet skirt. |
| *infra dig* | Archaeologist. |
| *in loco parentis* | In one's parent's train. |
| *in statu pupillari* | Contact lens. |
| *inter alia* | Domestic flights. |
| *intermezzo* | Between meals. |
| *intime* | At the right moment. |
| *jus contra bellum* | I am overweight. |
| *juste milieu* | Just a minute! |
| *karat* | Vegetable. |
| *kip* | Chicken. |
| *kipper* | Small chicken. |
| *laissez-faire* | Idle woman. |

| | |
|---|---|
| *lapsus memoriae* | Poor memory. |
| *largo* | Italian beer. |
| *legato* | Tailor's measurement. |
| *lemma* | Fruit drink. |
| *libido* | Bathroom fitting. |
| *libretto* | Type of sandal. |
| *lingua franca* | Speaking your mind. |
| *l'état c'est moi* | I am in a state. |
| *ma foi* | My liver. |
| *maladie* | Madam. |
| *mal vu* | Poor eyesight. |
| *mauvais goût* | Swollen leg. |
| *mis en page* | Slip of the pen. |
| *mistral* | Folk singer. |
| *négligé* | Careless. |
| *n'importe* | There is no port left. |
| *noblesse oblige* | Nobody will help. |
| *nom de plume* | Quill pen. |
| *non compos mentis* | Nonbiodegradable. |
| *nota bene* | Potato, or cabbage. |
| *nouvelle vague* | Modern novel. |
| *oeil-de-boeuf* | Oxtail soup. |
| *obscurum per obscuris* | You're standing in front of the light. |
| *odium* | A drug. |
| *odium theologicum* | Incense. |
| *palomine* | Friend of mine. |
| *par excellence* | Very good father. |
| *pas de deux* | Father of twins. |
| *passé* | Father has spoken. |
| *pax vobiscum* | Expression used by Italian waiters when tipping peas into your lap. |
| *polonaise* | Hay fever. |
| *post-obitum* | Earth re-entry. |
| *presto* | Tight shoe. |

| | |
|---|---|
| *rechauffé* | Rearrange. |
| *rentier* | Pay money to landlord. |
| *semper paratus* | Always a parrot. |
| *son et lumière* | Your son is smoking. |
| *sotto voce* | Slurred speech. |
| *sub poena* | Under the pony. |
| *table d'hôte* | Hot plate. |
| *terra cotta* | Fear of beds. |
| *terra incognita* | Fear of the unknown. |
| *tour de force* | Troop inspection. |
| *tour de main* | Palmistry. |
| *vice versa* | Limerick. |
| *vis-à-vis* | To return the insult. |
| *volte face* | Wooden horse. |
| *zweifellos* | Two men. |

## BON MOT

I think the last word on the subject belongs to Goethe: "Wer fremde Sprachen nicht kennt, weiss nichts von seiner eigenen."
    How true.

# LOVE, LOVE, LOVE!

They say it's love that makes the world go around. They also say that variety is the spice of life. On both counts I agree with them. I never tire of hearing the words "I love you", but now and again I like to be offered a variation on the theme. Here, drawn from real life and the movies, are eight of the more stirring declarations of love I've come across:

"I have seen only you, I have admired only you, I desire only you."
—Napoléon Bonaparte to Marie Walewska

"I was born when you kissed me, I died when you left me. I lived a few days when you loved me."
—Gloria Grahame to Humphrey Bogart in *In a Lonely Place*

"I love you soulfully and bodyfully, properly and improperly, every way that a woman can be loved."
—George Bernard Shaw to English actress Ellen Terry, with whom he had an epistolary romance

"I cannot live without my life ... I cannot love without my soul...."
—Laurence Olivier as Heathcliff after the death of Cathy in *Wuthering Heights*

"In thy face I have seen the eternal."
—Baron Christian von Bunsen to his wife as he lay dying

"Oh my Lolita! ... a ray of sunshine at the break of day! As a stream of light in an obscure night."
—No, not Nabokov, but Ludwig I of Bavaria to the dancer, Lola Montez

"I need your love as a touchstone of my existence. It is the sun which breathes life into me."
—Juliette Drouet to her lover Victor Hugo

"Don't ever think of the things you can't give me – You've trusted me with the dearest heart of all – and it's so damn much more than anybody else in all the world has ever had."
—Zelda Sayre to F. Scott Fitzgerald


## POWER FOR LUST

Perhaps people with a lust for power are more passionate than the rest of us. Certainly, for highly charged love letters, it would be hard to top these three – from Winston Churchill, Napoléon Bonaparte, and Eva Peron.

WINSTON CHURCHILL TO HIS WIFE, CLEMENTINE

France
September, 1919

My darling one
    Only these few lines to mark the eleventime we have seen the 12th Sept. together. How I rejoice to think of my gt good fortune on that day! There came to me the greatest

happiness and the greatest honour of my life....

My dear it is a rock of comfort to have yr love and companionship at my side. Every year we have formed more bonds of deep affection....

I can never express my gratitude to you for all you have done for me and for all you have been to me.

yr ever loving and devoted
W.

NAPOLEON BONAPARTE TO JOSEPHINE BEAUHARNAIS

February 1796
Seven o'clock in the morning
My waking thoughts are all of you. Your portrait and the remembrance of last night's delirium have robbed my sense of repose. Sweet and incomparable Joséphine, what an extraordinary influence you have over my heart. Are you vexed? Do I see you sad? Are you ill at ease? My soul is broken with grief and there is no rest for your lover....

But is there more for me when, delivering ourselves up to the deep feelings which master me, I breathe out upon your lips, upon your heart, a flame which burns me up? Ah! It was this past night I realised that your portrait was not you.

You start at noon. I shall see you in three hours. Meanwhile, mio dolce amor, accept a thousand kisses, but give me none, for they fire my blood.

EVA PERON TO HER HUSBAND, JUAN:

Flying to Europe
June 6th 1947
I am very sad to be leaving because I am unable to live away from you, I love you so much that what I feel for you is a kind of idolatory, perhaps I don't know how to show what I feel for you, but I assure you that I fought very hard in my life with the ambition to be someone and I suffered a great deal.

But then you came and made me so happy that I thought it was a dream and since I had nothing else to offer you but my heart and my soul I gave them to you wholly but in all these three years of happiness, greater each day, I never ceased to adore you for a single hour or thank Heaven for the goodness of God in giving me this reward of your love, and I tried at all times to deserve it by making you happy.

I don't know if I achieved that, but I can assure you that nobody has ever loved or respected you more than I have.

I am so faithful to you that if God wished me not to have you in this happiness and took me away I would still be faithful to you in my death and adore you from the skies. . . .

Many kisses, but many kisses. . . .

Evita.

## THE BROWNING VERSION

Some of the finest poetry in the English language has love as its central theme. Of all the great love poems my favourite is one of Elizabeth Barrett Browning's *Sonnets from the Portuguese:*

How do I love thee? Let me count the ways.
I love thee to the depth and breadth and height
My soul can reach, when feeling out of sight
For the ends of Being and ideal Grace.
I love thee to the level of every day's
Most quiet need, by sun and candle light.
I love thee freely, as men strive for Right;
I love thee purely, as they turn from Praise.
I love thee with the passion put to use
In my old griefs, and with my childhood's faith.
I love thee with a love I seemed to lose
With my lost saints – I love thee with the breath,
Smiles, tears, of all my life! – and, if God choose,
I shall but love thee better after death.

## BITTERSWEET

I am a sentimentalist. I like my love poetry sickly sweet. A verse like this one, sent by Dorothy Parker to her husband who was fighting in the 1914/18 War, I find almost too painful to bear.

> Only, for the nights that were,
> Soldier, and the dawns that came,
> When in sleep you turn to her,
> Call her by my name.

## LOVE AND MARRIAGE

Not all the poets who have celebrated love and marriage in their work have taken the subject as seriously or as sneeringly as did Mrs Browning or Mrs Parker. Look at these five verses, all written by men:

> I recollect a nurse called Ann,
> Who carried me about the grass,
> And one fine day a fine young man
> Came up, and kissed the pretty lass.
> She did not make the least objection!
> Thinks I "Aha!
> When I can talk I'll tell Mama,"
> —And that's my earliest recollection.
>
> FREDERICK LOCKER-LAMPSON

> When I was young and full of life
> I loved the local doctor's wife,
> And ate an apple every day
> To keep the doctor far away.
>
> THOMAS LAMONT

> 'Twas in a restaurant they met,
> Romeo and Juliet
> He had no cash to pay the debt,
> So Romeo'd while Juliet.
>
> VERNON NAISMITH

"Come, come," said Tom's father, "At your
    time of life,
There's no longer excuse for thus playing the rake—
It is time you should think, boy, of taking a wife."
"Why, so it is, father – whose wife shall I take?"

THOMAS MOORE

I have come to the conclusion
Having given it a test,
That of all my wife's relations,
I like myself the best.

HENRY ROBINSON

## LOVE ALL

Of all the great screen lovers, the greatest was undoubtedly Groucho Marx. Who could fail to be bowled over by lines like these?

"Send two dozen roses to Room 424 and put 'Emily I love you' on the back of the bill."

"Emily will you marry me – I will never look at another horse."

# MERRY CHRISTMAS

There's always been a Christmas.

That's not quite true. There's *almost* always been a Christmas. Certainly there was one long before Christ was born, though it wasn't called Christmas then. The deep midwinter has been a time for jollification and celebration for thousands of years, and even if Adam and Eve didn't hang out stockings in the Garden of Eden, many of the Christmas traditions we now take for granted began not so long after the Fall.

The Ancient Romans launched their week-long celebration of fire and light, the Saturnalia, on December 17th and quickly followed it up with three days of New Year festivities, called Kalends. In between, on December 25th itself, came the *Dies Natalis Invicti Solis* – the Birthday of the Unconquered Sun – sacred to Mithras, god of light, and to Attis, the Phrygian sun-god.

These Roman holidays may sound staid, but by all accounts the Saturnalia was a time when the Latins really let their hair down. It wasn't simply an excuse for indulging in the pleasures of wine, women, and song; it was also an opportunity for organized anarchy. Servants dressed up as their masters, lords pretended to be slaves, gentlemen danced drunkenly in the streets wearing little but blackened faces and animal skins. On a gentler level, special lamps were burned, special greenery was brought in to decorate the home, and special presents were exchanged.

The lights, the evergreens, and the gifts were also a feature of another pre-Christian midwinter romp: The Festival of Yule. On December 22nd, the time of the winter solstice when the sun is farthest from the Equator and at the point where it appears to pause before returning, the old Norsemen lit giant fires to the grim gods Odin and Thor, ate too much, drank too much, and wished one another a Very Merry Yuletide.

They weren't the only ones to use the winter solstice as a peg for a pagan party. The Druids chose the day for celebrating the Festival of Nolagh. The Greeks latched on to it as the birthday of Ceres, Hercules, and Bacchus. The Egyptians claimed it as the feast day of Horus, the son of Isis. And the list could go on and on because quite some time before the Christians decided that December 25th should be the birthday of Jesus, people from all over the world – from Greece and Rome, from Scandinavia and the Middle East, from India and China and South America – all had their own particular festivities at this time of year.

In fact, when Pope Julius I decided around the year 350 that Jesus' birthday should no longer be on January 1st or March 29th or September 29th but on December 25th, happily he chose a date that had always been associated with merrymaking. And, with a bit of luck, it always will be.


## THE MEANING OF CHRISTMAS

The history of Christmas apart, do you know its true meaning? Now that I've checked it out in every dictionary I can think of I believe I do. There's more to the word than you'd imagine. According to a wide range of reliable authorities, Christmas is:

1 an annual church festival kept on December 25th or by the Armenians on January 6th in memory of the birth of Christ, celebrated generally by a particular church service, special gifts and greetings, and observed in most Christian communities as a legal holiday.

2 any similar festivity or revelry.

3 the Christmas season.

4 the festival season from Christmas Eve till after New Year's or (especially in England) till Epiphany.

5 Christmas Day, December 25th.

6 the Christmas holidays.

7 something connected with the celebration of Christmas, as a gift.

8 any gift or present bestowed at Christmastime.

9 Christmas decorations.

10 evergreens used for decorations at Christmas, as the European holly.

11 the holly, *Ilex aquifolium.*

12 something special to drink at Christmastime.

13 a Texan term for whisky.

14 a cake made on Christmas Eve.

15 any ostentatious display, as of clothing, jewellery, etc.

16 garish article of clothing or jewellery, or one that sparkles.

17 a shower of metallic foil dropped by an aeroplane or released from an artillery shell to jam enemy radar or communications systems.

18 a mild, euphemistic expletive.

19 payday.

20 a baptismal name, now uncommon as a boy's name and practically unknown as girl's.

21 a frequent surname for one born near Christmas.

22 the surname of Gerard Christmas, an English carver who died in 1634.

23 the surname of Henry Christmas, an English writer who lived from 1811 until 1868.

24 a surname that appears over forty times in the London telephone directory.

25 a town in Gila County, Arizona.

26 a town in Orange County, Florida.

27 a town in Alger County, Michigan.

28 a lake in Hennepin County, Minnesota.

29 a place in Bolivar County, Mississippi.

30 a town in Morgan County, Tennessee.

31 a mountain in the Antarctic, at 82 degrees south, 159 degrees east.

32 a British island in the Indian Ocean about 190 miles south of Java.

33 one of the Line Islands in the central Pacific Ocean south of Hawaii, being the largest atoll in the Pacific.

34 a verb meaning "to celebrate Christmas".

35 an obsolete verb meaning "to provide with Christmas cheer".

36 a verb meaning "to decorate with evergreens for Christmas".

37 a verb meaning "to sell Christmas decorations".

38 a verb meaning "to adorn with Christmas decorations".

39 a verb meaning "to spend Christmas".

40 a verb, short for *Christmas Eve,* that is rhyming slang for "to believe".

41 a verb meaning "to engage in sexual activity".

So now you know what it's all about, have a cool Yule.

# N
## EVER SAY DIE

Never say die if you've got more than one of them. *Dice* is the plural of *die*.

The English language is rich in curious words that have even curiouser plurals. Here's an A to Z of some of them. They can all be found in *Webster's Third New International Dictionary*.

| SINGULAR | PLURAL |
| --- | --- |
| Adai | Adaize |
| brother | brethren |
| Chetty | Chettyars |
| Dukhobor | Dukhobortsky |
| englyn | englynion |
| Feis | Feiseanna |
| goosefoot | goosefoots |

| | |
|---|---|
| holluschick | holluschickie |
| iter | itinera |
| juger | jugera |
| Kuvasz | Kuvaszok |
| landsman | landsleit |
| mongoose | mongooses |
| never-was | never-weres |
| ornis | ornithes |
| paries | parietes |
| quadrans | quadrantes |
| rubai | rubaiyat |
| shtetl | shtetlach |
| tenderfoot | tenderfoots |
| ulcus | ulcera |
| vila | vily |
| wunderkind | wunderkinder |
| Xhosa | Amaxhosa |
| yad | yadayim |
| zecchino | zecchini |

Having given you twenty-six curious plurals each beginning with a different letter of the alphabet, let me give you another twenty-six, each *ending* with a different letter of the alphabet.

| SINGULAR | PLURAL |
|---|---|
| vas | vasa |
| chub | chub |
| calpul | calpullec |
| squid | squid |
| bildungsroman | bildungsromane |
| riff | riff |
| hog | hog |
| matzo | matzoth |
| jajman | jajmani |
| Bhumij | Bhumij |

| | |
|---|---|
| puli | pulik |
| court-martial | courts-martial |
| seraph | seraphim |
| torte | torten |
| buffalo | buffalo |
| sheep | sheep |
| Qaraqalpaq | Qaraqalpaq |
| krone | kroner |
| plural | plurals |
| matzo | matzot |
| ushabti | ushabtiu |
| Pshav | Pshav |
| mother-in-law | mothers-in-law |
| plateau | plateaux |
| pince-nez | pince-nez |

## SINGULAR QUIZ

Here are twenty-five everyday words. Can you give the plural for each of them?

| | | | |
|---|---|---|---|
| 1 | axe | 14 | oboe |
| 2 | ox | 15 | cherub |
| 3 | son-in-law | 16 | crisis |
| 4 | potato | 17 | datum |
| 5 | piccolo | 18 | cannon |
| 6 | attorney general | 19 | addendum |
| 7 | lieutenant colonel | 20 | agenda |
| 8 | opus | 21 | phenomenon |
| 9 | index | 22 | madam |
| 10 | teaspoonful | 23 | pelvis |
| 11 | mister | 24 | paymaster general |
| 12 | man-of-war | 25 | brigadier general |
| 13 | manservant | | |

(See Answers, page 267.)

# O LL KORRECT, OK?

Too much nonsense has been talked about the expression *OK*. I'm here to set the record straight, and I intend to be quick about it. OK?

*OK* does *not* come from the Choctaw word *oke* meaning "it is" or from *hoke* meaning "yes".

*OK* does *not* come from the practice of grading words for furniture making, the best oak of course being *Oak A*.

*OK* does *not* come from the O.K. Club named after Old Kinderhook, Martin Van Buren's birthplace.

OK, are you ready for the truth? In New England 150 or so years ago there was a craze for abbreviations, and *OK* and *O.K.* first appeared in print in various Boston newspapers, along with many other abbreviations. *R.T.B.S.* was "remains to be seen". *S.P.* was "small potatoes". *O.F.M.* was "our first men". Inevitably a number of the abbreviations had to be explained for the benefit of uninitiated readers. E.g., The *Boston Morning Post* of June 12th 1838 spoke of "a duel W.O.O.O.F.C. (with one of our first citizens)". The craze went so far as to produce abbreviations of intentional misspellings. *N.G.* for "no go" and *A.R.* for "all right" gave way to *K.G.* for "know go," and *O.W.* for "oll wright". *OK* for "oll korrect" followed quite naturally. And of all the varied and colourful abbreviations and misspellings of the time, it alone spread and survived.

So now you know, OK?

# PARDON ME!

## MY MISTAKE

Mrs Beverly Nina Avery, of Los Angeles, California, has been divorced sixteen times ... the Decca recording company said "No" to the Beatles because they thought they were too old-fashioned ... Demolition experts in Baltimore, Maryland, recently razed a two-storey house to the ground and then discovered it was the wrong one ... *The New York Times* once ran a headline that read "Judge Acts to Keep Theater Open" ... and not long ago I came across this inscription on a tombstone:

Sacred to the memory of
MAJOR JAMES BRUSH
who was killed by
the
accidental discharge
of a pistol by
his orderly
14th of April 1831.
Well done thou good and
faithful servant.

Like it or not, believe it or not, we all make mistakes. Indeed, mistake-making is one of the very few factors that can honestly be said to unite mankind.

As a writer prone to making mistakes, I'm in excellent company. There have been not-so-deliberate slips in some of the greatest masterpieces of world literature. For example, in Daniel Defoe's novel *Robinson Crusoe* the shipwrecked hero decides to salvage some goods from his ship before it sinks completely. Defoe describes how Crusoe removes all his clothes before swimming to the ship, but forgetting this fact he allows him to fill his pockets with biscuits once he is on board!

And Sir Arthur Conan Doyle gave Sherlock Holmes's side-kick, Dr Watson, one war wound – but in two places. In *A Study in Scarlet* the wound is in the shoulder, while in *The Sign of Four* it is in Watson's leg.

## MEET THE PRESS

We all make mistakes, but some of us make more than others. The world's press is rightly noted for its ability to misquote, misprint, and misunderstand absolutely everything. If you've ever had anything to do with an event that's been written up by the press, I guarantee there was at least one error in the report. There's no point in sulking about it: face life as it is and make the most of it. After all, misprints like these – all taken from actual newspaper reports – can add a little extra something to a story.

"The landlord insisted that no female should be allowed in the bra without a man."

"Miss Patricia Muddleton, qualified vice instructor, sang *Christian, Dost Thou See Them?* on Sunday night."

"Mrs Alsop was married before anaesthetics came into use in surgical operations."

"I never went through that ghastly adolescent phase most girls experience. I went from child to woman in one go. One day I was a child. The next, a man."

"Mrs Freda Wallace Brown, 79, of Baltimore, Md., dined this week at her home. Service and cremation will be held next Thursday at 2:00 P.M."

"Never throw away old chicken bones, or those left from a roast. Put them in water and boil them for several hours with a few diced vegetables, it will make very delicious soap."

"The bride was gowned in white silk and lace. The colour scheme of the bridesmaids' gowns and flowers was punk."

"The accident occurred at Hillcrest Drive and Santa Barbara Avenue as the dead man was crossing the intersection."

"An Arab country, like Ireland, is a place where the remarkable seldom happens, and the impossible is of frequent occurrence."

"Many students are planning to follow the team to the scene of the bottle."

"Mr Bromsgrove suffered a stroke on 24 November 1980 but with the loving care of his family and his kind and efficient nurse, he never fully recovered."

"The ladies of the Helping Hand Society enjoyed a swap social on Friday evening. Everybody brought along something they no longer needed. Many of the ladies were accompanied by their husbands."

"Over 50 children took advantage of the mobile clinic and were examined for tuberculosis and other diseases which the clinic offered free of charge."

"The new bride is approximately eighteen feet wide from buttress to buttress."

"We note with regret that Mr Willis Overing is recovering after a serious car crash."

"The new hospital extension will enable patients to be prepared and served in such a way that has previously been impossible."

"Some of the boy's methods are quite ingenious, the professors at the Institute have found. For instance, when asked to multiply 20 by 24 mentally, he gave the answer – 600 – in a few seconds."

"Sex and violence came into Jane Morgan's life gradually. Then she became a Christian and matters escalated."

"Ms Turner has set up a campaign against incestuous relationships at the house where she loves with her parents."

"The city which claims to have the largest outdoor mule market in the world recently held a parade of asses led by the governor."

"Blend sugar, flour, and salt. Add egg and milk, cook until creamy in double boiler. Stir frequently. Add rest of ingredients. Mix well and serve chilled. Funeral service will be held Thursday afternoon at two o'clock."

"An off-licence was looted and police opened fire after they were stoned."

"Before the girls left the White House, Mrs Reagan presented each of them with a small engraving of the Execution Mansion to keep as a memento."

"We apologise for the error in last week's paper in which we stated that Mr Arnold Smith was a defective in the police force. This was a typographical error. We meant, of course, that Mr Smith is a detective in the police farce, and are sorry for any embarrassment caused."

## HITTING THE HEADLINES

These headlines have all appeared in English-speaking newspapers around the world. It's true I promise.

MAN FOUND DEAD IN GRAVEYARD

LOCAL MAN HAS LONGEST HORNS IN TEXAS

PASSENGERS HIT BY CANCELLED TRAINS

BUFFALO SWEPT OFF FEET BY MENDELSSOHN CHOIR

MASSIVE ORGAN DRAWS THE CROWD

HAMM FAILS TO IDENTIFY YEGGS

SISTERS WED BROTHERS HAVE BABIES SAME DAY

POLICE MOVE IN BOOK CASE

UNDERTAKER'S FAILURE – LET DOWN BY CUSTOMERS

20-YEAR FRIENDSHIP ENDS AT THE ALTAR

NEWLY WEDS AGED 82, HAVE PROBLEM

LUCKY MAN SEES FRIENDS DIE

BACHELORS PREFER BEAUTY TO BRAINS IN THEIR WIVES

PRISONERS ESCAPE AFTER EXECUTION

MORE MEN FOUND WEDDED THAN WOMEN

FATHER OF TEN SHOT DEAD (MISTAKEN FOR RABBIT)

DEAD POLICEMEN IN THE FORCE FOR 18 YEARS

"LENORE" ONLY OPERA BEETHOVEN WROTE ON MONDAY EVENING

PROTESTOR TRIED TO SPOIL PLAY BUT THE ACTORS SUCCEEDED

# Q WITHOUT U

The world of words is full of surprises. For example, if you thought words beginning with the letter *Q* always had to have *U* as their second letter, you were wrong. Here are thirty that don't:

| | |
|---|---|
| *qabbala* | A system of occult theosophy or mystical interpretation of the Scriptures. |
| *qadi* | A Muslim judge who interprets and administers the religious laws of Islam. |
| *qaf* | The twenty-first letter of the Arabic alphabet. |
| *qaid* | A Muslim local administrator. |
| *qaimaqam* | A lieutenant or deputy in the service of the Ottoman Empire. |
| *qanat* | An underground tunnel dug in hills to convey water to plains below. |
| *qaneh* | A Hebrew measurement equivalent to 10.25 feet. |

| | |
|---|---|
| *qantar* | Any of various units of weight in Mediterranean countries. |
| *qasab* | An ancient measure of Arabia equivalent to 12.6 feet. |
| *qasida* | A satiric poem in various related Oriental cultures. |
| *qcepo* | A skin infection. |
| *qebhsnauf* | A hawk-headed son of the ancient Egyptian god Horus. |
| *qhat* | An obsolete spelling of *what*. |
| *qhwom* | An obsolete spelling of *whom*. |
| *qhythsontyd* | An obsolete spelling of *Whitsuntide*. |
| *qiana* | The trade name of a washable and wrinkle-resistant fabric related to nylon. |
| *qibla* | The direction of the Kaaba shrine in Mecca toward which all Muslims turn in ritual prayer. |
| *qinah* | A dirge or lament. |

And here are thirty more words culled from a variety of English dictionaries. They all contain the letter *Q*, but again it isn't followed by a *U*, except in the case of *zaqqum*, which is the only word in the language that manages to have it both ways.

| | |
|---|---|
| *bathqol* | A divine revelation audibly given. |
| *burqa* | A loose enveloping garment worn in public by Muslim women. |
| *cinq* | The number five in dice or cards. |
| *cinqfoil* | Any of several plants. |
| *coq* | A trimming of cock feathers on a woman's hat. |
| *faqih* | A Muslim theologian versed in the religious laws of Islam. |
| *faqir* | A Muslim ascetic. |
| *fiqh* | In Islam, jurisprudence based on theology. |
| *fuqaha* | A plural of *faqih*, above. |
| *hooqqa* | A pipe for smoking tobacco. |
| *Iraqi* | A native or inhabitant of Iraq. |
| *iraqize* | To make Iraqi in character. |

| | |
|---|---|
| *miqra* | The Hebrew text of the Bible. |
| *muqaddam* | A headman. |
| *nastaliq* | An Arabic script used mainly for Persian poetry. |
| *paq* | A large rodent of Central and South America. |
| *pontacq* | A still wine of the south of France, red or white. |
| *sambuq* | A small Arab boat. |
| *shoq* | An East Indian tree. |
| *shurqee* | A southeasterly wind of the Persian Gulf. |
| *suq* | A marketplace. |
| *taluq* | A subdivision of a revenue district in India. |
| *taluqdar* | A landholder. |
| *taqlid* | Uncritical and unqualified acceptance of a traditional orthodoxy. |
| *tariqah* | The Sufi path of spiritual development. |
| *trinq* | A toast, used in Rabelais's *Pantagruel*. |
| *waqf* | The granting of property in trust for a pious purpose. |
| *yaqona* | A beverage made from the crushed root of an Australasian shrubby pepper. |
| *zaqqum* | An infernal tree with excessively bitter fruit, mentioned in the Koran. |
| *zindiq* | A heretic characterized by an extreme religious infidelity to Islam. |

# RIGHT OR WRONG?

### THE FACTS OF LIFE

Can you face facts?

Can you bear to accept that when you thought you were right you were wrong all along?

Can you cope with the news that there is no soda in soda water, that rats don't desert a sinking ship, that Charles Lindbergh wasn't the first man to fly the Atlantic, and that Marie Antoinette of France never said "Let them eat cake"?

You can? Well, then you're probably strong enough to read on and discover how mistaken so many of our most cherished beliefs turn out to be.

There is no soda in soda water. It is charged with carbon dioxide like other "sparkling" drinks.

Rats don't desert a sinking ship. They are unable to predict disaster, and so if a ship happens to sink they will go down with it.

Charles Lindbergh was not the first person to fly nonstop across the Atlantic. He was the sixty-seventh, although he was the first to do it alone.

Marie Antoinette did not say "Let them eat cake." The phrase was attributed to her by those in opposition to Louis XVI and first gained currency thirty years before when Jean-Jacques Rousseau had a princess declare "Let them eat brioches" in a fictitious story of his.

The goosestep is not a German invention. It was introduced by the British Army. A commanding officer devised the step to enable him to see if any of his men were drunk.

An ostrich does not bury its head in the sand when it is frightened or wants to hide. It only does so when it is covering its eggs for protection or searching for food.

Mustard gas is not a gas; neither is it mustard. It is a volatile liquid.

There is no rice in rice paper. It is made from pitch or wood pulp.

Camel's hair brushes are not made from camel's hair but from squirrel's hair.

A pineapple is not a pine or an apple. It is a berry. And a potato is neither a vegetable nor a fruit. It is a root.

Spaghetti did not originate in Italy but came from China. It was introduced to Italy in the thirteenth century by the explorer Marco Polo.

"A red rag to a bull" is meaningless – because bulls are colour blind.

The Emperor Nero did not fiddle while Rome burned. Fiddles had not been invented, and at the time of the fire he was fifty miles away at his villa.

There is no scientifically sound reason for baiting mousetraps with cheese. Mice like food of all sorts and have no special preference for cheese.

Chop suey isn't a Chinese dish. It originated in California.

Wormwood is not a wood; neither is it a worm. It is an aromatic plant.

Snakes cannot be charmed by music because they have no ears and are deaf to music. However, they can feel vibration, and so it is possible that they respond to a snake charmer's foot tapping rather than his music.

The centipede doesn't have a hundred legs; it usually has twenty-one or thirty, though some have more than one hundred. And millipedes certainly don't have a thousand legs; very few have more than two hundred.

It's a mistake to say the moon shines. It doesn't. It has no light of its own and so only reflects the light of the sun.

## DON'T QUOTE ME

### Can you tell who said what?

1 I can't understand what's holding up our missile program. It's the first time the government ever had trouble making the taxpayer's money go up in smoke.
Bob Hope or Alan Alda?

2 You have to be a Republican to know how good it is to be a Democrat.
Jimmy Carter or Jacqueline Kennedy?

3 Humanity is acquiring all the right technology for all the wrong reasons.
R. Buckminster Fuller or Aleksandr Solzhenitzyn?

4 Hollywood's a place where they'll pay you a thousand dollars for a kiss, and fifty cents for your soul.
Joan Baez or Marilyn Monroe?

5 I'm an instant star, just add water and stir.
David Bowie or Dudley Moore?

6 Love is more important than what we can take ... Please say with me, three times – Love! Love! Love!
Pelé or Paul McCartney?

7 It takes two to destroy a marriage.
Margaret Trudeau or Bianca Jagger?

8 Today's "fact" becomes tomorrow's "misinformation".
Alvin Toffler or Isaac Asimov?

9 I'm fed up to the ears with old men dreaming up wars for young men to die in.
George McGovern or John F. Kennedy?

10 We all live under the same sky, but we don't all have the same horizon.

Mao Tse-tung or Konrad Adenauer?

11 Macho does not prove mucho.
Germaine Greer or Zsa Zsa Gabor?

12 The world is full of willing people, some willing to work, the rest willing to let them.
Robert Frost or Margaret Thatcher?

13 Falling madly in love with someone is not necessarily the starting point to getting married.
Prince Charles or Joan Collins?

14 You're never too old to become younger.
Mae West or George Burns?

15 The question isn't at what age I want to retire, it's at what income.
George Foreman or Muhammad Ali?

16 When I was kidnapped my parents snapped into action: they rented out my room.
Woody Allen or Lenny Henry?

17 No one's free, even the birds are chained to the sky.
Bob Dylan or Ted Hughes?

18 Television has changed the American child from an irresistible force into an immovable object.
David Frost or Laurence Peter?

19 Pop music is the hamburger of every day.
Leonard Bernstein or Pierre Boulez?

20 In your heart, you know I'm right.
Barry Goldwater or Barry Manilow?

(See Answers, page 268.)

# S WEET AND SOUR

### SWEET

When Marlene Dietrich complained to a photographer that the pictures he'd just taken of her weren't as good as the ones he'd taken of her when they'd last met, he replied: "Well, I'm ten years older than when I first photographed you, Miss Dietrich." That's what I call a compliment – inspired, instantaneous, ingratiating.

In the middle of the last century a French government clerk, charged with the responsibility of issuing passports, found himself confronted by a woman whose dazzling beauty was unsurpassed in his experience. Instead of noting the details of her height, the colour of her eyes and hair, her distinguishing marks, and so on, in describing her, he simply wrote: "More like an angel than a woman."

And there is the more recent story of the young man who was applying for entry to the naval college at Dartmouth. Asked by the interviewing admiral to name three distinguished officers of the Royal Navy, the applicant replied, "Sir Francis Drake, Admiral Horatio Nelson and ... I didn't quite catch your name, sir?"

As you can tell, I collect compliments, even when they are paid to others:

JOHN SPARROW ON MAURICE BOWRA

Without you, Heaven would be too dull to bear,
And Hell will not be Hell if you are there.

ASTRONAUT SCOTT CARPENTER TO MARLENE DIETRICH

I have been into space, I have been to the bottom of the sea, but I have never been as moved as by you tonight.

JOHN COCTEAU ON BALLET DANCER IDA RUBINSTEIN

She looks like the pungent perfume of some exotic essence.

HENRY JAMES, SR., ON HIS DAUGHTER ALICE

I never saw one so fitted by her grace and playfulness of wit to adorn this life.

CHARLES DICKENS TO WASHINGTON IRVING

What pleasure I have had in seeing and talking with you, I will not attempt to say. I shall never forget it as long as I live.

OLIVER WENDELL HOLMES TO JULIA WARD HOWE ON HER SEVENTIETH BIRTHDAY

To be seventy years young is sometimes far more cheerful and hopeful than to be forty years old.

JOHN ROBINSON, SPEAKER OF THE VIRGINIA HOUSE OF BURGESSES, TO GEORGE WASHINGTON

Your modesty is equal to your valour, and that surpasses the power of any language I possess.

ROSSINI ON BACH

If Beethoven is a miracle of humanity, Bach is a miracle of God.

KATE CHOPIN ON FELLOW WRITER RUTH MCENERY STUART

Her voice in conversation ... has a melting quality that penetrates the senses, as some soothing ointment goes through the skin. Her eyes do the rest – complete the charm begun by voice, expression, and a thoroughly natural and sympathetic manner. ... She is a delightful, womanly woman.

JOHN F. KENNEDY ON THOMAS JEFFERSON, AT A DINNER FOR NOBEL PRIZE WINNERS

I think this is the most extraordinary collection of talent, of human knowledge, that has ever been gathered together in the White House – with the possible exception of when Thomas Jefferson dined alone.

## SOUR

Emerson was right: "Every sweet hath its sour, every evil its good."

OSCAR LEVANT ON DORIS DAY

I knew her before she was a virgin.

JANET FLANNER ON SOCIETY HOSTESS ELSA MAXWELL

She has never been any closer to life than the dinner table.

COCO CHANEL ON YVES SAINT LAURENT

Saint Laurent has excellent taste. The more he copies me, the better taste he displays.

TRUMAN CAPOTE ON JACK KEROUAC'S WORK

That's not writing, that's typing!

WOOLLCOTT ON PROUST

Reading Proust is like bathing in someone else's dirty bathwater.

### MARK TWAIN ON JANE AUSTEN

Jane Austen's books, too, are absent from this library. Just that one omission alone would make a fairly good library out of a library that hadn't a book in it.

### OSCAR WILDE ON JAMES WHISTLER

Popularity is the only insult that has not been offered Mr. Whistler.

### WILLIAM WILDE ON BROTHER OSCAR

Oscar is not a man of bad character; you could trust him with a woman anywhere.

### GRAHAM GREENE ON FRED ASTAIRE

The nearest we are likely to get to a human Mickey Mouse.

### PHILIP GUEDALLA ON HENRY JAMES

The work of Henry James has always seemed divisible by a simple dynastic arrangement into three reigns: James I, James II, and the Old Pretender.

### BILLY WILDER TO CLIFF OSMOND (AFTER HEARING HIM SING)

You have Van Gogh's ear for music.

### ART BUCHWALD ON JIMMY CARTER

I worship the very quicksand he walks on.

### GRACE SLICK ON TRICIA NIXON

The worst thing a little acid could do to Tricia Nixon is turn her into a merely delightful person instead of a grinning robot.

# T
## HERE WAS A YOUNG LADY ...

There was a young lady named Zanka
Who retired while the ship lay at anchor;
> But awoke in dismay
> When she heard the mate say:
"We must pull up the top sheet and spanker."

A limerick, as you probably know, is a five-line nonsense verse that originated with the eighteenth-century ale-house chorus "Will you come up to Limerick." As a form of poetry it was made famous by Edward Lear.

Although at the limericks of Lear
We may be tempted to sneer
> We should never forget
> That we owe him a debt
For his work as the first pioneer.

The trouble with Lear's limericks is that they tend to be remarkably respectable.

> There was an old person from Twickenham
> Who whipped his four horses to quicken 'em;
> > When they stood on one leg
> > He said faintly "I beg
> We may go back directly to Twickenham!"

And the trouble with respectable limericks is that they tend to be somewhat short on laughs.

> The limerick packs laughs anatomical
> Into space that's quite economical
> > But the good ones I've seen
> > So seldom are clean
> And the clean ones so seldom are comical.

I wanted to offer you my choice of the world's top ten limericks, but given that *The Joy of Lex* is designed for family reading, finding ten printable ones hasn't been easy.

> The limerick form is complex
> Its contents run chiefly to sex.
> > It burgeons with virgeons
> > And masculine urgeons
> And swarms with erotic effects.

In making my selection I've done my best to find limericks that are both decent and amusing. After all, in poetry – as in fancy dress – it's subtlety that counts.

> There was a young woman from Aenos
> Who went to a party as Venus.
> > We told her how rude
> > 'Twas to go there quite nude,
> So we got her a leaf from the green-h'us.

If any of the ten I've chosen give offence, I apologize. MY sole aim has been "to give delight and hurt not ".

> A girl who weighed many oz.
> Used language I dare not pronoz.
> > For a fellow unkind
> > Pulled her chair out behind
> Just to see (so he said) if she'd boz.

There was a young maid from Madras
Who had a magnificent ass.
      Not rounded and pink
      As you probably think –
It was grey, had long ears, and ate grass.

Said an envious erudite ermine:
"There's one thing I cannot determine;
      When a girl wears my coat
      She's a person of note:
When I wear it I'm only called vermin."

Said a cat as he playfully threw
His wife down a well in Peru,
      "Relax, dearest Thora,
      Please don't be angora,
I was only artesian you."

There was a young peasant named Gorse
Who fell madly in love with his horse.
      Said his wife: "You rapscallion
      That horse is a stallion –
This constitutes grounds for divorce."

There was a young girl known as Sue
Who carried a frog in each shoe.
   When I asked her to stop
   She replied with a hop
"I'm trying to get in Who's Zoo!"

A newspaper man named Fling
Could make "copy" from any old thing.
      But the copy he wrote
      Of a five-dollar note
Was so good he is now in Sing Sing.

There was a young woman named Bright
Whose speed was much faster than light.
      She set out one day,
      In a relative way,
And returned on the previous night.

A cheerful old bear at the Zoo
Could always find something to do.
      When it bored him, you know
      To walk to and fro,
He reversed it, and walked fro and to.

God's plan made a hopeful beginning,
But man spoiled his chances by sinning.
    We trust that God's Glory
    Will end up the story
But at present the other side's winning!

# U RSULA WOOP AND FRIENDS

### REAL NAMES

Ursula Woop is alive and well and living in East Germany where she recently became National Typewriting Champion.

Adolph Blaine Charles David Earl Frederick Gerald Hubert Irvin John Kenneth Lloyd Martin Nero Oliver Paul Quincy Randolph Sherman Thomas Uncas Victor William Xeres Yancy Zeus Wolfeschlegelsteinhausenbergerdorffvoralternwarengewissenhaftschafterswessenschafewarenwohlgepfflegtundsorgfaltigkeitbeschutzenvonangreifendurcheinenanderersteerdemenschderraumschiffgebrauchlichtalsseinursprungvonkraftgestaltseinlangefahrthinzwischensternartigraumaufdersuchenachdiesternewelchegehabtbewohnbarplanetenkreisedrehensichundwohinderneuerassevonverstandigmenschlichkeitkonnte-

fortpflanzenundsicherfreuenanlebenslanglichefreudeundruhem-
itnichteinfurchtvorangreifenvonanderenintelligenzengeschopfs-
vonhinzwischensternartigraum, Senior, is alive and well and
living in Philadelphia where he has taken to calling himself Mr
Wolfe + 585, Sr., for short.

The world is full of ordinary people with quite extraordinary names. Here are fifty of them, all alive and well and living
somewhere in the United States, Canada, or Britain.

| | |
|---|---|
| Eve Adam | Bent Korner |
| Etta Apple | Joseph Wood Krutch |
| Philip Brilliant | Hunt A. Lusk |
| Betty Burp | Spanish McGee |
| Upson Downs | Asa Miner |
| Luscious Easter | Savage Nettles |
| Ophelia Egypt | Belle Nuddle |
| Alice Everyday | Elly Oops |
| Wanda Farr | Victor Overcash |
| Lo Fat | Ure A. Pigg |
| Thaddeus Figlock | Freeze Quick |
| Yetta Gang | Wanton Rideout |
| Solomon Gemorah | Pious Riffle |
| Bess Goodykoontz | Viola Rubber |
| Henry Honetchurch Gorringe | Bea Sharpe |
| Fair Hooker | Bess Sinks |
| Rutgers I. Hurry | Adelina Sloog |
| Melvin Intriligator | Verbal Snook |
| Frank Ix | Daily Swindle |
| Hannah Isabell Jelly | Ophelia Tittey |
| Amazing Grace Jones | Brutus Twitty |
| Love Joy | Viola Unstrung |
| Even Keel | Thereon Yawn |
| Pleasant Kidd | Homer Yook |
| Royal Knights | Fuller Zest |

## Identity crisis

Edward Banks, Leonard Douglas, William Elliott, Don Reynolds, and Leonard Spaulding are one and the same man: Ray Bradbury. It is not unusual for authors to adopt different pen names for books written in differing styles, but few eminent writers can have assumed as many *noms de plume* as this distinguished gentleman:

Mr Brown
Groley Byles
Folkstone Canterbury
John Corks
Fitzroy Clarence
Jeames de la Pluche
Frederick Haltamont de Montmorency
Henry Esmond, Esq.
Boldomero Espertero
The Fat Contributor
George Savage Fitz Boodle, Esq.
Major Goliah Gahagan
A Gentleman in Search of a Man-servant
M. Gobemouche
Leontius Androcles Hugglestone
Jeames of Buckley Square
Theresa MacWhorter
Master Molloy Molony
Mulligan of Kilballymulligan
One of Themselves
Arthur Pendennis
Peter Perseus
Harry Rollicker
The Honourable Wilhelmina Amelia Skeggs
Ikey Soloms, Esq., Junior

    Miss Tickleboty
    Michael Angelo Titmarsh
    Lancelot Wagstaff
    Theophile Wagstaff
    Charles James Yellowplush

What was his real name?

(See Answers, page 268.)

## Split personalities

Showfolk – from Julie Andrews to John Wayne – have been changing their names for generations. Miss Andrews started life as Julia Elizabeth Wells and the Duke was known as Marion Morrison as a child.

Here are the real names of twenty-five more stars of stage, screen and concert platform. Some are late and lamented, others are alive and kicking. By which names are they better known?

    Betty Perske
    Lesley Hornby
    Robert Zimmerman
    Annie Mae Bullock
    Maurice Micklewhite
    Frank J. Cooper
    Bernard Schwartz
    Francesca Mitzi Marlene de Charney von Gerber
    Archibald Leach
    Harlean Carpenter
    Reginald Dwight
    Roy Fitzgerald
    Maurice Cole
    Allen Konigsberg
    Robert Davies
    Sofia Scicolone

Dino Crocetti

Maria de Carmo Miranda de Cunha

Estelle O'Brien Merle Thompson

Gladys Smith

Virginia McMath

George O'Dowd

Richard Starkey

Shirley Schrift

Sarah Jane Fulks

(See Answers, page 268.)

## FIND THE MAN

In the wonderful world of anagrams *a gentleman* is *an elegant man, a grand finale* is *a flaring end,* and *Adolf Hitler* is very properly *hated for ill.*

Here are anagrams of the surnames of twenty famous men – philosophers, kings, inventors, scientists, statesmen, and so on – from all periods of history. Can you name them:

| | |
|---|---|
| 1 tank | 11 onside |
| 2 coat | 12 inward |
| 3 linen | 13 snares |
| 4 prone | 14 uncate |
| 5 loons | 15 encase |
| 6 actors | 16 pasture |
| 7 radius | 17 amusers |
| 8 latins | 18 seamers |
| 9 epochs | 19 coasters |
| 10 hurtle | 20 puritans |

(See Answers, page 269.)

## FIND THE BOY

*He'll do in mellow verse* is an anagram of *Oliver Wendell Holmes* and a *person whom all read* is *Ralph Waldo Emerson*.

Can you unscramble these words and find fifty first names for boys?

| | |
|---|---|
| 1 rice | 26 maori |
| 2 vain | 27 spire |
| 3 lark | 28 sails |
| 4 lace | 29 roped |
| 5 line | 30 lynne |
| 6 lone | 31 grade |
| 7 mail | 32 grader |
| 8 vane | 33 nailed |
| 9 raze | 34 wander |
| 10 turk | 35 enters |
| 11 mile | 36 lardon |
| 12 smile | 37 sinned |
| 13 irene | 38 flared |
| 14 dolly | 39 glared |
| 15 ingle | 40 monies |
| 16 snide | 41 radian |
| 17 widen | 42 calmer |
| 18 cigar | 43 events |
| 19 nicol | 44 arnhem |
| 20 lyric | 45 ordain |
| 21 ducal | 46 antrim |
| 22 brain | 47 sorbet |
| 23 naiad | 48 fasten |
| 24 anvil | 49 yonder |
| 25 banal | 50 meager |

(See Answers, page 269.)

## FIND THE GIRL

*Had Indian rig* is an anagram of *Indira Gandhi* and *as a man, rejoined old France* is *Jeanne D'Arc, Maid of Orleans.*

Can you unscramble these words and find fifty first names for girls?

| | | |
|---|---|---|
| 1 gem | 18 ladle | 35 great |
| 2 yam | 19 daily | 36 aural |
| 3 hurt | 20 canny | 37 Maori |
| 4 road | 21 inane | 38 amble |
| 5 sore | 22 label | 39 issue |
| 6 soar | 23 fared | 40 hoard |
| 7 sets | 24 Alice | 41 osier |
| 8 teak | 25 Ernie | 42 breath |
| 9 army | 26 Lloyd | 43 threes |
| 10 sail | 27 Lenny | 44 airman |
| 11 lace | 28 Aidan | 45 Easter |
| 12 soil | 29 Colin | 46 monies |
| 13 lean | 30 asset | 47 Hamlet |
| 14 dean | 31 lilac | 48 riding |
| 15 dine | 32 ideas | 49 triads |
| 16 goal | 33 ideal | 50 singly |
| 17 coral | 34 Lethe | |

(See Answers, page 269.)

## COUNTRY NAMES

The names of some countries include within them a boy's or girl's name. For example, the name *Ada* forms part of Can*ada* and Gren*ada*.

Can you find names of countries in which the following personal names appear?

| | |
|---|---|
| 1 Guy | 8 Philip |
| 2 Stan | 9 Mark |
| 3 Dan | 10 Ken |
| 4 Don | 11 Les |
| 5 Alan | 12 Leo |
| 6 Gary | 13 Eli |
| 7 Rita | 14 Martin |

(See Answers, page 270.)

O, IS THAT ALL?

Yes, for people whose name it is.

In Burma there are people called U and E, but the most widely used single-letter surname in the world is simply O.

# V IOLINISTS ARE UNSTRUNG

## OCCUPATIONAL HAZARDS—FOR PUN-LOVERS

Violinists are unstrung.

Bankers are disinterested.

Butchers are delivered.

Models are denuded.

Songwriters are decomposed.

Castles are demoted.

Surveyors are dislocated.

Accountants are disfigured.

Witch doctors are dispelled.

Train drivers are derailed.

Symphony conductors are disconcerted.

Siamese twins are departed.

Diplomats are disconsolate.

Cannibal victims are disheartened.

Ministers are demoralized.

Orchestra leaders are disbanded.

Winemakers are deported.

Mathematicians are discounted.

Advertisers are declassified.

Martians are unearthed.

Admirals are abridged.

Tailors are unsuited.

Neurologists are unnerved.

Brides are dismissed.

Committee members are disappointed.

Electricians get discharged.

Authors are described.

Choristers are unsung.

Mathematicians are nonplussed.

Politicians are devoted.

Calendar makers are disMayed.

Hairdressers are distressed.

Tree surgeons are uprooted.

Prisoners are excelled.

Bridge players are discarded.

Teachers are outclassed.

Turkey stuffers are undressed.

Eulogists are distributed.

Puzzlers are dissolved.

Clubs are dismembered.

Private eyes are undetected.

Botanists are deflowered.

Tennis players are unloved and defaulted!

Arsonists are unmatched and fired!

Gunsmiths, they're just plain fired!

## NATIONAL OPUNIONS—FIVE OF A KIND

Hollywood's not-so-eternal triangles usually end up as wreck tangles.

You can always tell a baby from Alabama by its southern drool.

Seeing a brood of children playing outside a teepee on an Indian reservation, a visitor asked the father how many children he had. "Twenty-one," he answered her proudly.

"My, my," said the visitor. "Don't you have endless squabbles and fights and arguments?"

"Not at all," said the father. "We're just one big Hopi family!"

Following a major earthquake in California, a group of citizens set up the San Andreas Fund, which just goes to prove what they say about some Californians being generous to a fault.

Meet the man from Miami! If you think his jacket is florid, you should see his wife's: it's even Florida!

## PUN MOTS—TWENTY THAT SCORE

Alan F. G. Lewis is the world's premier punster. Here are twenty of his gems:

A Puritan is a man who noes what he likes.

He was like a bull in a china shop until she cowed him.

Slimmer's motto: here today, gaunt tomorrow.

The guru refused to let his dentist freeze his jaw because he wanted to transcend dental medication.

When I'm stoned I get a little boulder.

"You're always telling lice ant you mite bee found out," he ticked her off.

The hard part of being broke is watching the rest of the world go buy.

With games like Scrabble you won't get board, but the same's not true of Monotony.

Chalet or shanty? It's a decision we should dwell on.

Banging together brass plates in the orchestra isn't as cymbal as it looks.

Atrophy is a reward for long political service.

I've put my money into a new girlie magazine so I can take accrued interest.

A pessimist is a person who looks at the world through morose-coloured glasses.

The chemical name for water is $H_2$ eau.

Only a fool would milk his company of expenses when none has been in curd.

One man's Mede is another man's Persian.

Pity the poor man who has a big load of debt and doesn't know how to budge it.

The old Christmas spirit is like artificial holly: dead and berried.

I was neutral until a live wire promised me the earth.

The system of decimal notation has its point but fractions are often vulgar.

## JESTER STORY

A pun my soul, it can be a dangerous business this punning. Witness the story of the mediaeval court jester who was an inveterate punster and punned knight and day until his master, the monarch – an ace of a king and quite a card by all accounts – was driven beyond reason and ordered the fool to be carried away to the gallows, there to be strung up. No sooner had the jester been dragged from the royal presence than the king began to reflect on the problems of acquiring a replacement, and it didn't take long to have him sending a pardon speeding after the condemned jester.

The messenger carrying the pardon reached the gallows just in time to save the victim, who was already standing with the rope around his neck. The pardon proclaimed the jester's freedom on condition that he never cracked another pun in his life. But old habits die hard, and without thinking the jester promptly said: "No noose is good news."

And they hanged him.

# WASHINGTON SQUARE

If you take the surnames of all the Presidents of the United States and try to interlink them in the manner of a crossword you will need a grid with 527 squares. Here it is:

```
W A S H I N G T O N                               M
I     O     A                                     C
L     O     R           J A C K S O N       P O L K
S     V   F I L L M O R E     E           I       I
O     E   I   I         F   N I X O N   C A R T E R   N
N     R   E   N     T A F T   N         E   R       L
        L   C   E       E   E       J   C   E
      F O R D   O   M   R   D   A   M O N R O E     Y
  H         L   A   S   T Y L E R   H   O
V A N   B U R E N   D   O       T   N   O     C
  R   U       I   N         H A Y E S S       C
  D   C   T   S           U     O     E       O
  I   H A R R I S O N   T A Y L O R   N   V   L
  N   A   U       N         D       E   I
G R A N T   M         R E A G A N   C L E V E L A N D   G
    A     A         M           T         G
    N     N     E I S E N H O W E R         E
```

## WASHINGTON, PENNSYLVANIA

If you study a map of the United States, you will be able to find the names of all but one of the Presidents. For example, Abraham Lincoln is represented by the communities of Abraham, in Utah, and Lincoln, in Nebraska. The only gap is Eisenhower. There doesn't appear to be a community of that name anywhere in the United States, though you can find Ike in Texas.

Finding middle names for all the Presidents isn't possible, and in this respect President Truman presents a special problem. Harry S. Truman was his full name (the S. didn't stand for anything), but since the country doesn't seem to have a town called Harry, let alone one called S, the community of Harrys in Texas has had to serve for both of President Truman's first names. There isn't a town called Jimmy either, and so the thirty-eighth President appears more formally as James Earl Carter.

| | | |
|---|---|---|
| George (Arkansas) | | Washington (Pennsylvania) |
| John (Kentucky) | | Adams (California) |
| Thomas (West Virginia) | | Jefferson (Colorado) |
| James (Mississippi) | | Madison (Wisconsin) |
| James (Mississippi) | | Monroe (Utah) |
| John (Kentucky) | Quincy (Massachusetts) | Adams (Illinois) |
| Andrew (Iowa) | | Jackson (Mississippi) |
| Martin (Alabama) | | Van Buren (Ohio) |
| William (W. Virginia) | Henry (Idaho) | Harrison (Georgia) |
| John (Kentucky) | | Tyler (Texas) |
| James (Georgia) | Knox (New York) | Polk (Nebraska) |
| Zachary (Louisiana) | | Taylor (Arizona) |
| Millard (Wisconsin) | | Fillmore (Wyoming) |
| Franklin (New Jersey) | | Pierce (Florida) |
| James (Georgia) | | Buchanan (New Mexico) |
| Abraham (Utah) | | Lincoln (Nebraska) |
| Andrew (Iowa) | | Johnson (Kansas) |
| Ulysses (Nebraska) | Simpson (Indiana) | Grant (New York) |
| Rutherford (New Jersey) | | Hayes (South Dakota) |
| James (Georgia) | | Garfield (New Jersey) |

| | | |
|---|---|---|
| Chester (Virginia) | | Arthur (Nevada) |
| Grover (Wyoming) | | Cleveland (Ohio) |
| Benjamin (Alabama) | | Harrison (Idaho) |
| William (W. Virginia) | | McKinley (Wyoming) |
| Theodore (Alabama) | | Roosevelt (Oklahoma) |
| William (W. Virginia) | Howard (Rhode Island) | Taft (Kentucky) |
| Woodrow (Arkansas) | | Wilson (Connecticut) |
| Warren (Arizona) | | Harding (W. Virginia) |
| Calvin (Illinois) | | Coolidge (Texas) |
| Herbert (Missouri) | | Hoover (South Dakota) |
| Franklin (New Jersey) | | Roosevelt (Arizona) |
| Harrys (Texas) | | Truman (Minnesota) |
| Dwight (Kansas) | David (Kentucky) | ????? |
| John (Kentucky) | Fitzgerald (Georgia) | Kennedy (Wisconsin) |
| Lyndon (Vermont) | | Johnson (Florida) |
| Richard (Louisiana) | | Nixon (New Jersey) |
| James (Georgia) | Earl (Wisconsin) | Carter (Tennessee) |
| Ronald (Alabama) | | Reagan (Texas) |

# X!

FOR ADULTS ONLY

You are about to read the shortest poem in the history of world literature. It represents the elegiac cry of the poet – a censorious and half-starved ex-husband at the crossroads of life – when confronted with a plate of ten fried eggs that remind him of his former wife, their honeymoon in Rome, and the happy breakfasts they once shared.

The poem is untitled. Here it is:

X!

## BRIEF LIVES

Not so economical but marginally more profound is this little poem that asks a universal question:

> Must
> All this aching
> Go to making
> Dust?

Yes is the short answer.

The shortest poem to encapsulate the whole of human existence is probably this one:

> O life,
> O love,
> O pain,
> O joy,
> O death.

And the shortest single sentence to do the same thing must be this one from *Finnegans Wake* by James Joyce:

> They lived and laughed and loved and left.

I don't think there's much more to be said, do you?

# Y OUR TURN

### IT'S LAUGHABLE

Can you find an everyday English word of eight letters that contains four *G*s?

(See Answers, page 270.)

### IT'S FACETIOUS

*Abstemious* is a word in which the five vowels *A, E, I, O,* and *U* appear in alphabetical order. See if you can think of thirteen everyday English words containing the five vowels in these sequences:

```
A  I  E  O  U          E  U  O  I  A
O  E  A  U  I          E  U  A  I  O
A  U  I  O  E          I  A  O  U  E
A  I  O  U  E          O  A  U  I  E
E  O  U  A  I          O  U  E  A  I
I  O  U  A  E          U  A  I  O  E
                       U  O  I  A  E
```

(See Answers, page 270.)

## IT'S POINTLESS

Can you add the necessary punctuation to the sentence below to make sense of it?

THATTHATISISTHATTHATISNOTISNOTISNOTTHATITITIS

(See Answers, page 270.)

## IT'S INCOMPLETE

Here are twenty familiar five-letter words with uncommon endings. Can you supply the missing letters to complete the words?

```
* * R V A          * * N O M
* * V O C          * * X O M
* * M A D          * * I E N
* * U R D          * * F I N
* * A K I          * * M E D
* * A P I          * * L I O
* * O S K          * * R I O
* * K E L          * * L O O
* * R E M          * * S T O
* * X I M          * * L V O
```

Here are twenty familiar six-letter words with uncommon endings. Can you supply the missing letters to complete the words?

```
* * * O D A        * * * G E L
* * * H M A        * * * F I L
* * * R U B        * * * S U L
* * * H I D        * * * T H M
* * * I O D        * * * T I M
* * * U R D        * * * H O M
* * * E X E        * * * X E N
* * * A L F        * * * E M N
* * * U L F        * * * E B O
* * * Z O I        * * * C C O
```

Here are twenty familiar seven-letter words with uncommon endings. Can you supply the missing letters to complete the words?

```
* * * * O C A      * * * * P O O
* * * * A R B      * * * * R Z O
* * * * N A C      * * * * V A R
* * * * U A C      * * * * H U R
* * * * F F E      * * * * T A T
* * * * R R H      * * * * U B T
* * * * O T L      * * * * O C T
* * * * I E M      * * * * T S U
* * * * Z O N      * * * * R A X
* * * * R N O      * * * * M O X
```

(See Answers, page 270.)

## IT'S INCOMPREHENSIBLE

If you can understand that *CCCCCCC* represents the Seven Seas and *EHCA* gives you backache, you should be able to decipher these hieroglyphics.

1 POTOOOOOOOO        8 PPPOD

2 SYMPHON        9   C
                                GENT
                                 A

3 DNUOR

4 B      E      D        10 ONCE
                                  9 AM

5 BOLT
    TH                            11 CATN

6 FECDISTANT        12 <u>A REMAINDER</u>
                                    UR

7 REVILO

(See Answers, page 271.)

# Z EE END

## TOWARD THE END

Toward the end of their lives most people make a will. In his the German poet Heinrich Heine stipulated that in order to inherit his fortune his wife must remarry "so that there will be at least one man to regret my death."

Where there's a will there's often an insight into the life and character of the person whose will it is.

FROM THE LAST WILL AND TESTAMENT OF NAPOLEON BONAPARTE SIGNED AT ST. HELENA ON APRIL 15, 1821:

1 I die in the apostolical Roman religion, in the bosom of which I was born, more than fifty years since.

2 It is my wish that my ashes may repose on the banks of the Seine,

in the midst of the French people, whom I have loved so well.

3 I have always had reason to be pleased with my dearest wife, Marie Louise. I retain for her to my last moment, the most tender sentiments – I beseech her to watch, in order to preserve my son from the snares which yet environ his infancy.

4 I recommend to my son, never to forget that he was born a French prince, and never to allow himself to become an instrument in the hands of the triumvirs who oppress the nations of Europe; he ought never to fight against France, or to injure her in any manner; he ought to adopt my motto – "Everything for the French people".

5 I die prematurely, assassinated by the English oligarchy. .... The French nation will not be slow in avenging me.

FROM THE LAST WILL AND TESTAMENT OF ALFRED BERNHARD NOBEL SIGNED IN PARIS ON NOVEMBER 27, 1895:

The whole of my remaining estate shall be dealt with in the following way: The capital shall be invested by my executors in safe securities and shall constitute a fund, the interest on which shall be annually distributed in the form of prizes to those who, during the preceding year, shall have conferred the greatest benefit on mankind.

The said interest shall be divided into five parts, which shall be apportioned as follows: one part to the person who shall have made the most important discovery or invention within the field of physics; one part to the person who shall have made the most important chemical discovery or improvement; one part to the person who shall have made the most important discovery within the domain of physiology or medicine; one part to the person who shall have produced in the field of literature the most outstanding work of an idealistic tendency; and one part to the person who shall have done the most or the best work for fraternity among nations, and for the abolition or reduction of standing armies and for the holding and promotion of peace congresses.

It is my express wish that in awarding the prizes no consideration whatever shall be given to the nationality of the candidate, so that the most worthy shall receive the prize whether he be a Scandinavian or not.

Paris, November 27, 1895. Alfred Bernhard Nobel

THE WILL OF ONE WILLIAM HICKINGTON WHO DIED IN 1770:

> This is my last will,
> I insist on it still;
> To sneer on and welcome,
> And e'en laugh your fill.
>> I, William Hickington,
> Poet of Pocklington,
> Do give and bequeath,
> As free as I breathe,
> To thee, Mary Jarum
> The Queen of my Harum,
> My cash and my cattle,
> With every chattel,
> To have and to hold,
> Come heat or come cold,
> Sans hindrance or strife,
> Though thou art not my wife.
> As witness my hand,
> Just here as I stand,
> The twelfth of July
> In the year Seventy.

Wm. Hickington

THE WILL OF PHILADELPHIA INDUSTRIALIST WHO DIED IN 1947:

To my wife I leave her lover, and the knowledge that I wasn't the fool she thought I was.

To my son I leave the pleasure of earning a living. For twenty-five years he thought the pleasure was mine. He was mistaken.

To my daughter I leave $100,000. She will need it. The only piece of business her husband ever did was to marry her.

To my valet I leave the clothes he has been stealing from me for ten years. Also the fur coat he wore last winter while I was in Palm Beach.

To my chauffeur, I leave my cars. He almost ruined them and I want him to have the satisfaction of finishing the job.

To my partner, I leave the suggestion that he take some clever man in with him at once if he expects to do any business.

THE WILL OF EDWIN ORLANDO SWAIT WHO DIED IN 1965:

1 I direct that all my creditors be paid except my landlord.

2 I give and bequeath to my good friend, Theodore Weber, my best aluminium tin if I die of anything but indigestion. In that event, I give him a sad farewell.

3 To my old friend, Ann Lewis, I give and bequeath Purcell's "Passing By", which I wrongfully took and carried away last Christmas.

4 I give and bequeath to my dear friend, Mrs. George Hale, the satisfaction of being remembered in my will.

5 To my old pal, Mary Ledgerwood, I give and bequeath the sum of 35 cents. It's not much but it's the beginning of a Scotch fortune.

6 I leave to my lawyer, Huber Lewis, the task of explaining to my relatives why they didn't get a million dollars apiece.

7 I appoint Huber Lewis executor of my will. In view of his profession, I suppose we had better require him to furnish a bond. I give him full power to sell, mortgage or pledge any or all of my estate for the purpose of paying the legacy left by Article 5, and if a sufficient sum cannot be realized, I warn him to be wary of the legatee.

## AT THE END

At the end most people have something to say. Few could – or would want to – rival the Famous Last Words of General Sedgewick who peered over the parapet at Spotsylvania and remarked: "They couldn't hit an elephant at this dist——"

The only Famous Last Words that aren't essentially sad are the ones people dream up years before they are going to need them – like these:

GEORGE BERNARD SHAW

I knew if I stayed round long enough, something like this would happen.

RUBE GOLDBERG

Dear God: Enclosed please find Rube Goldberg. Now that you've got him, what are you going to do with him?

ROBERT BENCHLEY

This is all over my head.

ERNEST HEMINGWAY

Pardon me for not getting up.

FREDERIC MARCH

This is just my lot.

CLARK GABLE

Back to the silents.

DOROTHY PARKER

Excuse my dust.

LEWIS STONE

A gentleman farmer goes back to the soil.

HEDY LAMARR

This is too deep for me.

WILLIAM HAINES

Here's something I want to get off my chest.

WARNER BAXTER

Did you hear about my operation?

JEAN HARLOW

Of this quiet and peace
I'm very fond;
No more remarks – "She's a
Platinum blonde."

## AFTER THE END

After the end come the epitaphs. These all-American tombstone tributes are quite genuine.

Sacred to the memory of
Jared Bates
who died Aug. the 6th 1800.
His widow, aged 24, lives at 7 Elm
Street, has every qualification for
a good wife, and yearns to be comforted.

*Lincoln, Maine*

Here lies the body of our Anna
Done to death by a banana.
It wasn't the fruit that laid her low
But the skin of the thing that made her go.

*Enosburg, Vermont*

Here lies the body of Susan Lowder
Who burst while drinking a Seidlitz powder.
Called from this world to her Heavenly Rest
She should have waited till it effervesced. 1798.

*Burlington, New Jersey*

Here lies
Lester Moore
Four slugs
from a 44
no Les
no More

*Tombstone, Arizona*

In memory of
Mr Nath Parks, aged 19,
who on 21st March 1794 being out hunting
and concealed in a ditch was casually shot
by Mr Luther Frank.

*Elmwood Cemetery, Holyoke, Massachusetts*

To the four husbands of
Miss Ivy Saunders
1790, 1794, 1808, 18??
Here lies my husbands, One, Two, Three
Dumb as men could ever be.
As for the Fourth, well, praise be God,
He bides for a little above the sod.
Alex, Ben, Sandy were the first three's names,
And to make things tidy I'll add his – James.

*Shutesbury, Massachusetts*

Played five aces
Now playing the harp

*Boot Hill Cemetery, Kansas*

FINALLY

Let me echo Hilaire Belloc:

When I am dead, I hope it may be said:
"His sins were scarlet, but his books were read."

# ANSWERS

## X MARKS THE SPOT

### THE JOY OF LEX (page 30)

Apoplex, circumflex, complex, Culex, decemplex, duplex, exlex, flex, googolplex, hallex, ilex, implex, multiplex, octuplex, perplex, plex, pollex, proplex, Pulex, quadruplex, reflex, retroflex, scolex, silex, simplex, supellex, telex, triplex, Ulex, uncomplex

### COMPLEX ARRANGEMENTS (page 31)

Latex, lexicon, excelsior, exclude, dextral, exalted, explode, deluxe, axletree, flaxen, reflexly, sexology, helix, foxhole, lynxlike, extoll, maxwell, explain, explore, relaxed, petrosilex, latexes, phloxes, sexennial, larynxes, plexus, textural, sextile, sextuple, luxes

# WHAT'S IN A NAME?

## AN ORAL DANGER (page 40)

The names have been ordered in their so-called alphabetically reduced forms. For example, *Christiaan* and *Christiana* can both be "reduced" to *Aachiinrst*. If all the names are reduced in a similar way, and then these reduced forms are ordered alphabetically, that is the order of my list. Obviously, names with several *A*s come out at the top of the list, and names without any *A*s appear further down the list. Where a set of names has the same number of *A*s as another set, the tie is broken on the *B*s, *C*s, and so on.

## VERBIGERATION (page 42)

| | | | |
|---|---|---|---|
| 1 VV | 26 PP |
| 2 CC | 27 FF |
| 3 HH | 28 NN |
| 4 XX | 29 TT |
| 5 WW | 30 K |
| 6 Y | 31 V |
| 7 JJ | 32 C |
| 8 S | 33 H |
| 9 GG | 34 D |
| 10 KK | 35 A |
| 11 MM | 36 G |
| 12 LL | 37 O |
| 13 AA | 38 M |
| 14 Z | 39 J |
| 15 EE | 40 P |
| 16 DD | 41 W |
| 17 BB | 42 E |
| 18 OO | 43 F |
| 19 UU | 44 B |
| 20 SS | 45 Q |
| 21 QQ | 46 U |
| 22 RR | 47 N |
| 23 X | 48 I |
| 24 T | 49 R |
| 25 II | 50 L |

## MAKING A NAME IN THE STATES

CHICAGO (page 84)

At least thirty-four, including:

| | |
|---|---|
| Apkaw | Chikagons |
| Checago | Chikagou |
| Checagou | Chikagu |
| Cheegago | Chikagvv |
| Chegakou | Chikkago |
| Cheggago | Chirgago |
| Chekakou | Psceschaggo |
| Chicagou | Quadoge |
| Chicags | Schuerkaigo |
| Chicagu | Shecago |
| Chicagvv | Shercaggo |
| Chicago | Shikkago |
| Chicaqw | Stktschagko |
| Chiccago | Tschakko |
| Chigagou | Tzstchago |
| Chikag8 | Ztschaggo |

And just in case it looks as if the typographer has made a few mistakes, let me repeat four of the stranger spellings: Chicagvv, Chicag8, Chicaqw, and Ztschaggo.

## TEEN SENSE IN TENNESSEE (page 89)

| | |
|---|---|
| 1 San Antonito | 11 Savannah |
| 2 Bangor | 12 Hudson |
| 3 Casper | 13 Los Angeles |
| 4 Pontiac | 14 Salem |
| 5 Tucson | 15 Denver |
| 6 San Diego | 16 Laredo |
| 7 Madison | 17 Reno |
| 8 Detroit | 18 Las Vegas |
| 9 Notre Dame | 19 Toledo |
| 10 Reading | 20 New Carlisle |

### JUST A LINE (page 99)

1 Graham Greene: *The Power and the Glory*
2 Jean Paul Sartre: *Nausea*
3 Kurt Vonnegut: *Jailbird*
4 Daphne du Maurier: *Frenchman's Creek*
5 Ernest Hemingway: *Fiesta*
6 Charles Dickens: *Bleak House*
7 Franz Kafka: *The Trial*
8 John Steinbeck: *The Grapes of Wrath*
9 George Orwell: *1984*
10 Norman Mailer: *The Naked and the Dead*
11 L. P. Hartley: *The Go-Between*
12 Robert M. Pirsig: *Zen and the Art of Motorcycle Maintenance*
13 Agatha Christie: *Murder on the Orient Express*
14 Jack Kerouac: *On the Road*
15 Frederick Forsyth: *The Day of the Jackal*
16 Virginia Woolf: *The Voyage Out*
17 F. Scott Fitzgerald: *Tender Is the Night*
18 Laurence Sterne: *Tristram Shandy*
19 Gustave Flaubert: *Madame Bovary*
20 Leo Tolstoy: *Anna Karenina*

## I BEFORE E?

### A FINE SPELL (page 103)

It's *unbelievable*, of course. And the correct spellings for the other words follow:'

accommodation
battalion
broccoli
cemetery
Chihuahua
coliseum
connoisseur
coxswain

desiccate
ecstasy
eleemosynary
embarrass
fettuccine
gneiss
guillotine

haemorrhage
hypocrisy
idiosyncrasy
jubilee
kwashiorkor
liaison
liquefy
mischievous
moccasin
myrrh
naphtha
occurrence
paraffin
parallel
plausible
pseudonymous
quintessence

rarefy
reconnaissance
renaissance
sacrilegious
snagfroid
shillelagh
subpoenaed
supersede
threshold
ukulele
vermilion
vichyssoise
victual
weltschmerz
Xanthippe
yashmak
zabaglione

## CRAZY CROSSWORDS

THE WORLD'S SMALLEST CROSSWORD (page 120)

> PERIOD is the meaning of the clue ACROSS.
> DOT is the meaning of the clue DOWN.

AN AUSTRALIAN CROSSWORD (page 120)

N O O N

AN IRISH CROSSWORD (page 120)

P A T
A   A
T A P

As you can see the answer is decidely apt.

## Crazy crosswords

### A SIBILANT CROSSWORD (page 122)

### AN ANAGRAMMATIC CROSSWORD (page 124)

Correct solution first; then intermediate solution of across clues; then explanation of clue.

ACROSS

1 PSITTACINE, ANTISEPTIC (*ant is* + *t* inside *epic*)
6 LANE, LEAN (2 meanings)
10 CONICAL, LACONIC (*con* inside *laic*)
11 MIRACLE, RECLAIM (*rec, l, aim*)
12 SHRUB, BRUSH (2 meanings)
13 SENESCENT, SENTENCES (2 meanings)
14 TURBINATE, RESIDENT (*side in rent*)
15 PRESTO, POSTER (reverse of ret, sop)
17 PLATEN, PLANET (hidden stee*p lane t*here is)
19 RINGSIDE, DESIRING (*R.I.* inside anagram of *design*)
23 TURBINATE, TRIBUNATE (*N.A.* inside *tribute*)
25 INTER, NITER (*t* inside reverse of *rein*)
27 ENCLAVE, VALENCE (*Vance*, with *LE* inside)
28 TOILERS, LOITERS (*lo, i, ters* (e))
29 TONE, NOTE (2 meanings)
30 STRAIGHTEN, SHATTERING (*hatter* inside *sing*)

DOWN
1 PACES (*p, aces*)
2 IGNORES (anagram)
3 TICK-BORNE (anagram)
4 CELESTE (hidden in reverse of gre*ets elec*torate)
5 NAMING (*N. A. Ming*)
7 ARCHERS (*marchers*, minus first letter)
8 ELECTRODE (*elect, rode*)
9 KRIS (reverse of *sir, k*)
14 IMPATIENT (*I'm, patient*)
16 REGAINING (*E.G.* inside training, minus first letter)
18 AFRICAN (*FR I*, inside *a can*)
20 INERTIA (anag. of I train, e)
21 INTREAT (former version of *entreat: in, treat*)
22 LATEST (hidden inside stimu*lates t*rend)
24 IRAN (*I, ran*)
26 RISEN (anagram)

A CROSSWORD WITH MISPRINTS (page 126)

Correct answer first; then correct definition form; then explanation of clue.

ACROSS
1 CLEANER, char, (*C-leaner*)
5 CASTLED, fort (*cast, led*)
9 INFLEXION, bending (*flex*, with *in* first, and *I ON* afterwards)
10 RUN UP, erect, (first letters of Unionist Party after run)
11 BLUFFS, deceives (*b, luffs*)
12 PROVIDER, cater (*ID* inside *p, rover*)
14 INFLATES, swells (*in flats*, around *E*)
15 LEDGE, shelf (*Led*, first two letters of *geologists*)
18 TWEET, chirp (cf. *tweat, treat*)
20 PRESENTS, shows, (*present, s*)
23 EYEBALLS, stares (cf. *I, balls*)
25 ICE-CAP, cover (*I,C*, reverse of *pace*)
27 MORON, fool (*o* inside *morn*)
28 TRANSPIRE, sweat (anagram)
29 DESIRED, wanted (*sir* inside *deed*)
30 MASSEUR, stroker (*mass*, reverse of *rue*, Fr=street)

Actual answers first; then intermediary answers; then explanation of clue.

DOWN
1 CLIMBS, climes (*c, limes*)
2 EFFLUENCE, affluence (*flu* inside *a fence*)
3 NEEDFUL, heedful (*he*, anagram of *feud, l*)
4 RAID, rand (hidden in I*ran, d*ubiously)
5 CONTRASTED, contracted (2 meanings)
6 SHRIVEL, shriven (anagram of *shiver* + last letter in *absolution*)
7 LINED, lived (*devil, reversed*)

8 DEPORTED, reported (2 meanings)
13 STIPULATED, stimulated (*stated*, around *I MUL(e)*)
16 DETECTIVE, defective (*defect + I've*)
17 STREAMED, streaked (2 meanings)
19 TRAINER trailer (2 meanings)
21 ENCASES encages (first letter of *ghosts* inside anagram of *seance*)
22 UPREAR uproar (*U* pro *A.R.*)
24 EARNS warns (*n* inside *wars*)
26 FARM, firm (2 meanings)

### FLUID CROSSWORD (page 121)

P U N C H

P U N C H

P U N C H

P U N C H

P U N C H

The crossword is fluid because punch is also drink made with fruit juices, sugar and spices, often with wine or spirits added. The name comes from the Hindi *panch*, meaning five, the original number of ingredients.

# ANGELICAL ASPIRATES (page 141)

E
TE
ATE
TATE
STATE
ESTATE
RESTATE
PRESTATE

## BAA BAA BANANA!

### SEEING DOUBLE (page 148)

| | |
|---|---|
| A | *bazaar* |
| B | *ebb* |
| C | *accord* |
| D | *add* |
| E | *fee* |
| F | *off* |
| G | *egg* |
| H | *withhold* |
| I | *skiing* |
| J | *hajji* (a pilgrim to the tomb of Mohammed at Mecca) |
| K | *trekking* |
| L | *all* |
| M | *rummy* |
| N | *inn* |
| O | *boo* |
| P | *apple* |
| Q | *zaqqum* (an infernal tree with bitter fruit) |
| R | *err* |
| S | *ass* |
| T | *butt* |
| U | *vacuum* |
| V | *flivver* |
| W | *powwow* |
| X | *xx-disease* (a disease of cattle, also called hyperkeratosis) |
| Y | *gayyou* (a narrow, flat-bottomed boat) |
| Z | *buzz* |

### GIRL TALK (page 167)

1 Marilyn Monroe
2 Golda Meir
3 Martin Luther
4 Franklin P. Jones
5 Socrates
6 Thomas Beecham

7 Sigmund Freud
8 Susan B. Anthony
9 Dwight D. Eisenhower
10 Clare Boothe Luce
11 Peter De Vries
12 Gail Sheehy
13 Cornelia Otis Skinner
14 Hermione Gingold
15 Jane Fonda
16 Adela Rogers St. John
17 John Kenneth Galbraith
18 Jacqueline Kennedy Onassis
19 Simone de Beauvoir
20 Fran Lebowitz

## INTERNATIONAL SCRABBLE (page 178)

|   | | WORDS | | NO. OF POINTS |
|---|---|---|---|---|
| 1 | USA | GALERES } | with G on the double-letter square | 70 |
|   | USA/UK | REGALES } | | 70 |
| 2 | USA | ELATERS/AE/EL/NA/IT/AE/ER | | 74 |
|   | UK | STEALER/ST/TA/EE/AN/LI/EA/RE | | 75 |
| 3 | USA | PARADOX/RAPE/DOILY/OM/XI | | 173 |
|   | UK | PARADOX/ZO/EX | | 153 |
| 4 | USA | JOG/OH/GONE | | 53 |
|   | UK | ZHO/ZOA | | 67 |
| 5 | USA | JANIZARY/LATHER | | 115 |
|   | UK | JANIZAR/JOWL/NOPAL | | 177 |
| 6 | USA | BIOLOGIC/OWED | | 63 |
|   | UK | GNOTOBIOLOGICAL/OGEE/OWED/AH/ LAMBLING | | 684 |

## NEVER SAY DIE

### SINGULAR QUIZ (page 206)

1 axes

2 oxen

3 sons-in law

4 potatoes

5 piccolos
6 attorneys general
7 lieutenant colonels
8 opera
9 indices
10 teaspoonfuls
11 messrs.
12 men-of-war
13 menservants
14 oboes
15 cherubim or cherubin

16 crises
17 data
18 cannon
19 addenda
20 agenda *
21 phenomena
22 mesdames
23 pelves
24 paymasters general
25 brigadier generals

*Strictly speaking *agend* is the singular of agenda, but nowadays *agenda* is often used as the singular and *agenda* or *agendas* are both considered acceptable as plurals.

## RIGHT OR WRONG?

### DON'T QUOTE ME (page 219)

1 Bob Hope
2 Jacqueline Kennedy
3 R. Buckminster Fuller
4 Marilyn Monroe
5 David Bowie
6 Pelé
7 Margaret Trudeau
8 Alvin Toffler
9 George McGovern
10 Konrad Adenauer

11 Zsa Zsa Gabor
12 Robert Frost
13 Prince Charles
14 Mae West
15 George Foreman
16 Woody Allen
17 Bob Dylan
18 Laurence Peter
19 Pierre Boulez
20 Barry Goldwater

## URSULA WOOP AND FRIENDS

### IDENTITY CRISIS (page 231)

William Makepeace Thackeray

### SPLIT PERSONALITIES (page 232)

| Lauren Bacall | was | Betty Perske |
| Twiggy | was | Lesley Hornby |
| Bob Dylan | was | Robert Zimmerman |

| Tina Turner | was | Annie Mae Bullock |
|---|---|---|
| Michael Caine | was | Maurice Mickelwhite |
| Gary Cooper | was | Frank J. Cooper |
| Tony Curtis | was | Bernard Schwartz |
| Mitzi Gaynor | was | Francesca Mitzi Marlene de Charney von Gerber |
| Cary Grant | was | Archibald Leach |
| Jean Harlow | was | Harlean Carpenter |
| Elton John | was | Reginald Dwight |
| Rock Hudson | was | Roy Fitzgerald |
| Kenny Everett | was | Maurice Cole |
| Woody Allen | was | Allen Konigsberg |
| Jasper Carrott | was | Robert Davies |
| Sophia Loren | was | Sofia Scicolone |
| Dean Martin | was | Dino Crocetti |
| Carmen Miranda | was | Maria de Carmo Miranda de Cunha |
| Merle Oberon | was | Estelle O'Brien Merle Thompson |
| Mary Pickford | was | Gladys Smith |
| Ginger Rogers | was | Virginia McMath |
| Boy George | was | George O'Dowd |
| Ringo Starr | was | Richard Starkey |
| Shelley Winters | was | Shirley Schrift |
| Jane Wyman | was | Sarah Jane Fulks |

FIND THE MAN (page 233)

1 Kant 2 Cato 3 Lenin 4 Peron 5 Solon 6 Castro 7 Darius 8 Stalin 9 Cheops 10 Luther 11 Edison 12 Darwin 13 Nasser 14 Canute 15 Seneca 16 Pasteur 17 Frasmus 18 Rameses 19 Socrates 20 Rasputin

FIND THE BOY (page 234)

1 Eric 2 Ivan 3 Karl 4 Alec 5 Neil 6 Noel (or Leon) 7 Liam 8 Evan 9 Ezra 10 Kurt 11 Emil 12 Miles 13 Ernie 14 Lloyd 15 Nigel 16 Denis 17 Edwin 18 Craig 19 Colin 20 Cyril 21 Claud 22 Brian 23 Aidan 24 Alvin 25 Alban 26 Mario 27 Piers 28 Silas 29 Pedro 30 Lenny 31 Edgar 32 Gerard 33 Daniel 34 Andrew 35 Ernest 36 Ronald (or Roland or Arnold) 37 Dennis 38 Alfred 39 Gerald 40 Simeon 41 Adrian 42 Marcel 43 Steven 44 Herman 45 Dorian 46 Martin 47 Osbert 48 Stefan 49 Rodney 50 Graeme

FIND THE GIRL (page 235)

1 Meg 2 May (or Amy) 3 Ruth 4 Dora 5 Rose 6 Rosa 7 Tess 8 Kate 9 Mary (or Myra) 10 Lisa 11 Clea 12 Lois 13 Lena 14 Edna 15 Enid 16 Olga 17 Carol 18 Della 19 Lydia 20 Dancy 21 Annie 22 Bella 23 Freda 24 Celia 25 Irene 26 Dolly 27 Lynne 28 Diana 29 Nicol 30 Tessa 31 Cilla 32 Sadie 33 Delia 34 Ethel 35 Greta 36 Laura 37 Moira

38 Mabel 39 Susie 40 Rhoda 41 Rosie 42 Bertha 43 Esther (or Hester) 44 Marian (or Marina) 45 Teresa 46 Simone 47 Thelma 48 Ingrid 49 Astrid 50 Glynis

### COUNTRY NAMES (page 235)

1 Guyana 2 Afghanistan or Pakistan 3 Jordan or Sudan 4 Indonesia 5 New Zealand 6 Hungary 7 Mauritania 8 Philippines 9 Denmark 10 Kenya 11 Lesotho 12 Sierra Leone 13 Belize 14 Martinique

## YOUR TURN

### IT'S LAUGHABLE (page 247)

*Giggling*

### IT'S FACETIOUS (page 247)

Here are the most obvious solutions:

| | |
|---|---|
| AIEOU | *ambidextrous* |
| OEAUI | *overhauling* |
| AUIOE | *cautioned, auctioned* |
| AIOUE | *anxiousness* |
| EOUAI | *encouraging* |
| IOUAE | *discourage, inoculate* |
| EUOIA | *pneumonia, euphoria, sequoia* |
| EUAIO | *reputation, refutation, equation* |
| IAOUE | *dialogue* |
| OAUIE | *consanguine* |
| OUEAI | *housemaid* |
| UAIOE | *ultraviolet* |
| UOIAE | *unsociable* |

### IT'S POINTLESS (page 248)

That that is, is; that that is not, is not; is not that it? It is!

### IT'S INCOMPLETE (page 248)

#### FIVE-LETTER WORDS

larva, havoc, nomad, gourd, khaki, okapi, kiosk, yokel, harem, maxim, venom, buxom, alien, elfin, cameo, folio, curio, igloo, gusto, salvo

#### SIX-LETTER WORDS

pagoda, asthma, cherub, orchid, period, absurd, annexe, behalf, engulf, borzoi, cudgel, fulfil, consul, rhythm, victim, fathom, flaxen, solemn, gazebo, stucco

SEVEN-LETTER WORDS
tapioca, rhubarb, almanac, bivouac, giraffe, catarrh, axolotl, requiem, horizon, inferno, shampoo, scherzo, samovar, sulphur, habitat, redoubt, concoct, jujitsu, anthrax, flummox

## IT'S INCOMPREHENSIBLE (page 249)

1 potatoes
2 unfinished symphony
3 roundabout
4 bedspread
5 thunderbolt
6 disinfectant
7 Oliver Twist
8 two peas in a pod
9 undercover agent
10 once upon a time
11 tin can
12 You are under arrest.

All Futura Books are available at your bookshop or newsagent, or can be ordered from the following address: Futura Books, Cash Sales Department, P.O. Box 11, Falmouth, Cornwall TR10 9EN.

Please send cheque or postal order (no currency), and allow 60p for postage and packing for the first book plus 25p for the second book and 15p for each additional book ordered up to a maximum charge of £1.90 in U.K.

B.F.P.O. customers please allow 60p for the first book, 25p for the second book plus 15p per copy for the next 7 books, thereafter 9p per book.

Overseas customers including Eire please allow £1.25 for postage and packing for the first book, 75p for the second book and 28p for each subsequent title ordered.